Leveraging Good Will

Alice Korngold

Leveraging Good Will

Strengthening Nonprofits
by Engaging Businesses

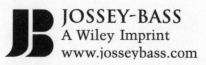
JOSSEY-BASS
A Wiley Imprint
www.josseybass.com

Published by Jossey-Bass
A Wiley Imprint
989 Market Street, San Francisco, CA 94103-1741   www.josseybass.com

Jossey-Bass books and products are available through most bookstores. To contact Jossey-Bass directly call our Customer Care Department within the U.S. at 800-956-7739, outside the U.S. at 317-572-3986, or fax 317-572-4002.

Jossey-Bass also publishes its books in a variety of electronic formats. Some content that appears in print may not be available in electronic books.

Library of Congress Cataloging-in-Publication Data
Korngold, Alice.
  Leveraging good will : strengthening nonprofits by engaging businesses /
Alice Korngold ; foreword by Melissa A. Berman.
    p. cm.
  Includes bibliographical references and index.
  ISBN-10: 0-7879-7361-0 (alk. paper)
  ISBN-13: 978-0-7879-7361-2 (alk. paper)
  1. Nonprofit organizations—United States—Management. 2. Nonprofit
organizations—United States—Finance. I. Title.
  HD62.6.K667 2005
  658.1'59—dc22
                                      2005007769

Printed in the United States of America
FIRST EDITION
HB Printing 10 9 8 7 6 5 4 3 2 1

Contents

For my beloved Gerry
David
Ethan, Ellie, and Gabriel
Omi and Opa

Foreword

Leveraging Good Will: Strengthening Nonprofits by Engaging Businesses
comes at a critical time, as sweeping developments force us to re-
frame how we define the effectiveness of these mission-driven organizations. What are these developments? First, doubts about
nonprofit accountability have been building in the press, the public sector, and the general public over the past few years—fueled by
confusion and anger about notable scandals involving questionable
compensation and benefits, misuse of donations, loose controls on
overseas funding, and astonishing ratios of fundraising expenses to
program-related expenses. The Senate, the House, the U.S. Trea-
sury Department, the Internal Revenue Service, and the states
(especially California and New York) have all reacted by proposing
increased regulation or oversight. Trust in nonprofits has not yet
recovered from the controversies surrounding giving after 9/11.
Regardless of how pervasive the abuses are, the nonprofit sector risks
being redefined by its worst-case examples. Too many view nonprofits as inherently wasteful entities that offer questionable tax
advantages to donors and do little to serve the general public.

Second, and more broadly, approaches to assessing the effectiveness of nonprofits have multiplied. Enormous amounts of raw
data are now available, thanks to innovations like Guidestar's website. Several organizations are developing rating systems along the
lines of Standard and Poor's or Moody's. Venture philanthropy

groups have pioneered the use of venture-capital methods and reporting systems.

The stakes are high for assessing donations as social investments. At the simplest and most personal level, if we only knew which nonprofits really worked, we'd all be able to make better choices. (Of course, many of us will continue to support our alma mater even if its archrival is deemed more effective, but that's another story.) More significantly, objective information about results would mean that huge numbers of dollars could flow to the best of the best. As a result we'd quickly see solutions and a better world. Many observers are convinced that the funding streams for the social sector would both function better and be far deeper if we had a firm handle on effectiveness. If only we could measure return on investment (ROI) in these organizations and move away from giving toward investing, the floodgates of funding would open, and capital would flow downhill to initiatives with the highest ROI.

But bottom line and ROI are misleading analogies for the nonprofit sector in many cases. Only a few corners of the nonprofit world can show real return—generally those where transaction creates an immediate solution: providing inoculations; building a school; registering voters; legally protecting acres of land. But the complexity of the challenge is no excuse for not responding: nonprofits need to be able to show that they are both using their resources effectively and being effective in their sphere of activity.

This scrutiny is in fact having a helpful effect on the nonprofit sector. The focus on accountability is encouraging many nonprofits to take governance seriously, to seek board members who will actually read the audit report, and to provide board members with meaningful information. The focus on effectiveness is leading nonprofits to articulate the solution they offer, not just the depth of the problem they're addressing.

Paradoxically, as nonprofits work to find the best ways to assess and report on their effectiveness, they lack support from those who should help them in this complex process. The atmosphere of mistrust means that more donors and watchdogs than ever want nonprofits to place all their resources into programs, as opposed to administration, and donors increasingly put restrictions on their gifts to ensure that "overhead" isn't funded. Part of the pressure comes from a natural frustration over the fact that many nonprofits can't explain their cost structure or how they achieve results. Part of it comes from something more like wishful thinking—a hope that nonprofits can achieve their missions unencumbered by the realities of everyday life. Board members, especially those from the business sector, should help make the case that these demands can be short-sighted—that, in fact, they are less likely to lead to good programs than giving that recognizes the important of sound infrastructure. Businesspeople understand the difference between waste and operating expenses, and they know that organizations that don't invest in management and in systems may not last long.

But good nonprofit board members are made, not born. Often, businesspeople have barriers to overcome before they can be effective board members. At the simplest level, misunderstandings arise about terms and "code words" in the nonprofit sector. In business, *development* might refer to training and *capacity* to factory output. In the nonprofit sector, *development* is code for sales and marketing, while *capacity* can mean anything from ability to the equivalent of output. Second, businesspeople often misperceive how nonprofits operate and get funded—reporting requirements for nonprofits create some bizarre budget categories, for example. In some cases, disdain for those who don't come from the business sector leads businesspeople to assume that anyone from their world is smarter and more effective than anyone from the social sector.

Worst of all, many board members accept a role as the loyal sales force, campaigners for the cause and the organization regardless of results or reality. They check their logic at the door, cheering loudly as the nonprofit's management turns board meetings into sales meetings. Questions become a sign of disloyalty, and board members shrug off their responsibilities—abetted by management, which fears alienating major supporters. Sadly, nonprofit leaders are often smart to fall into this pattern. Board members may well be their biggest funders and may not want to hear about anything but success—or the increasing need for the nonprofit's wonderful programs. It's a pernicious cycle but one that board members and nonprofits can escape if they recognize that good nonprofit governance entails focusing on how the nonprofit accomplishes its mission, not just on how the checks get written. That's why the perspectives and tools in this book are so important. With sound preparation, businesspeople on boards can help nonprofits meet the challenges and opportunities of our troubled times with sophisticated, efficient solutions.

March 2005   Melissa A. Berman
                                President and CEO
                                Rockefeller Philanthropy Advisors, Inc.

Preface

Nonprofit organizations provide us and our communities with daily sustenance of food, shelter, protection against disease, pain, and suffering, and spiritual manna. Every day, we partake in the goods and services of nonprofit organizations as we stroll through parks, visit museums, see our physicians, drop off our children at day care, take college and graduate school courses, and visit our parents in nursing homes. Nonprofit organizations facilitate the building of parks, neighborhoods, and vibrant city centers. One needs only wander the streets of San Francisco, with its extraordinary public spaces, featuring marvelous sculptures and public concerts, to appreciate how compelling these benefits are for commercial and residential development and thus economic vitality. Nonprofit organizations also give us the means to nourish our souls, decide what matters, and find our path in life. We receive from nonprofit services a multitude of benefits that enrich our personal lives while also fostering civic and economic development.

Nonprofit organizations constitute a key sector of the nation's economy in addition to providing many of the most vital community services. A total of 1.2 million nonprofits employ eleven million workers in the United States. Nonprofits employ three times the number of people in agriculture and two times the number of employees in wholesale trade. Nonprofits employ almost 50 percent more people than construction, finance, insurance, and real estate combined. By adding in the volunteer labor force in the nonprofit sector, nonprofit employment climbs to 16.6 million, a figure that approaches that of all branches of manufacturing combined (20.5 million). Nonprofit revenues total $670 billion, 8.8 percent of the nation's gross national product (Salamon, 2004, p. 22).

Today's nonprofit sector is shaken to the core by financial and strategic threats. Changes in funding and expectations for nonprofits are forcing the sector to reinvent itself while also juggling the day-to-day demands and needs of the community. This book will advance the nonprofit sector by showing organizations how to lever-age the time and talents of highly qualified volunteers; such leverag-ing can happen now that individuals and their employers are beginning to realize how much satisfaction people derive from vol-unteer service. Nonprofits have a new advantage as businesses begin to understand the value of encouraging and supporting the involvement of their employees in community service. Today, busi-nesses understand that they can foster leadership development, team building, a company's image, and the vitality of the commu-nities where their employees and customers live and work. The ris-ing interest among businesses in involving themselves and their people in community service presents a fresh, new opportunity for nonprofits to access tremendous volunteer resources. Nonprofit organizations can leverage the vast resources of businesses to help transform their revenue models, operating practices, and strategic alliances. This book provides a brand-new road map for nonprofit organizations: a way to strengthen governance and improve orga-nizational effectiveness by drawing on valuable business talent and resources. This book provides a clear plan for using the renaissance of volunteerism to benefit volunteers, their employers, nonprofits, and the community.

Although business leaders clearly support the notion of com-munity involvement, the experience is too often frustrating for busi-nesses and volunteers as well as for nonprofits. This book goes beyond presenting the case for business involvement by providing direction for nonprofits seeking to engage businesses in productive and meaningful service. This book is for nonprofit organizations that want to increase their effectiveness and viability; it also addresses the interests of businesses seeking to be strategic and effective in strengthening communities; nonprofit resource centers and consulting firms, which can be strong connectors of businesses and nonprofits; and academic centers and teachers of courses in leadership development, business involvement in service, and nonprofit governance and management.

The book begins by making the case for nonprofits to engage business volunteers in high-impact organizations. Although businesses recognize the benefits of community involvement, their energies tend to be focused on large-scale, all-day volunteer marathons that make a great show. Yet businesspeople can play a far more meaningful role in helping nonprofits by bringing valuable skills, expertise, and relationships to the sector through board participation and volunteer management assistance. In order to be useful, however, businesspeople need to learn how to "make the translation"—apply their business acumen in the unique nonprofit environment. Moreover, nonprofit resource centers can add great value by matching business volunteers with nonprofit organizations and by providing ongoing coaching and consulting services to nonprofits and their business volunteers.

It has been an extraordinary experience for me to create nonprofit board-development services—including successful matching programs—for the benefit of hundreds of organizations; this has been my occupation for thirteen years, following fifteen years as a nonprofit entrepreneur and consultant to health care institutions and universities. For the purpose of leveraging good will, I have worked with a talented team to assist over 150 businesses and employers in focusing their community-involvement strategies for increased impact; we have devised a successful approach to training and then placing more than one thousand business executives and professionals on almost three hundred nonprofit boards. The key to good board placement is matching candidates based on their interests and qualifications, as well as the particular needs of each nonprofit. Most board members who have been placed through this process have risen to board leadership positions, thereby proving the quality of the matches and the importance of ongoing coaching and consulting. Most significantly, this approach to matching can be funded entirely by businesses and is thus free for nonprofits. In 1999, the *Wall Street Journal* featured the benefits of this successful approach in a front-page article (Langley, 1999). In 2003, John Bridgeland, director of USA Freedom Corps and special assistant to President George W. Bush, heralded this approach to effective nonprofit-board involvement as a model for all businesses and communities (Ruiz Patton, 2003). With support from the Charles Stewart Mott Foundation and the Carnegie Corporation, I am assisting a number of U.S. cities in adopting best practices in nonprofit-board matching.

We stand at the crossroads where businesses and nonprofits meet. From my vantage point, businesses have a great deal to offer and nonprofits need useful assistance, but the relationship requires careful brokering in order to make it a win-win for all parties and, most important, for the community. The businesspeople I work with say, "I've always wanted to get involved, but I never knew how and where." For their part, nonprofits know they need help, but they often do not trust businesspeople. Unfortunately, the nonprofits' worst fears are sometimes realized when well-meaning businesspeople are not thoughtfully matched or prepared. An effective nonprofit matchmaker can make it easy for businesspeople to connect where they will be most useful and can provide new volunteers with the necessary preparation and coaching. When the volunteer is involved in a project that touches the heart, then the volunteer's contribution and dedication can be leveraged to achieve meaningful results. Nonprofits must learn how to capitalize on the special talents of businesspeople. When the interests of businesses and non-profits are aligned, the impact can be tremendous. This book includes numerous accounts of businesspeople who have had a sub-stantial impact on the nonprofits where they served.

Having attended over twenty college and graduate school com-mencement ceremonies (my children's, those at Pace University, where I worked, and those at Case Western Reserve University School of Law, where my husband is dean), I have noticed that graduation speakers usually give the one and only important speech, the speech about "the rules of life." This speech focuses on honesty, integrity, and public service—what Peter Gomes, Harvard Univer-sity's chaplain, refers to as "the good life" (2002). The speaker and the life he or she has led make each speech unique and powerful. Speakers who have devoted themselves to public or community ser-vice as leaders in the civil rights movement, advocates for abused children, and scientific researchers who have helped understand and prevent or cure diseases carry serious weight with the audience. The message is powerful because the speaker has committed a lifetime to a cause that is meaningful. Our personal life choices distinguish each of us and make us credible role models for our children. When people are recognized at public events, they are not praised for the amount of money they have made or the houses they live in, but rather for their community service.

This is an extraordinary moment in time: the good will of busi-nesses and the talents of individuals seeking to serve can be lever-aged to transform nonprofit governance and management. The involvement of businesses can help ensure the success and long-term viability of critical health and human services, educational institutions, civic development initiatives, and cultural organiza-tions. If action is not taken now, then businesses and nonprofits will become discouraged and lose interest in each other. Now is the time to seize this golden opportunity to bring businesses and nonprofits together by taking a positive and productive approach. With a commitment to improve opportunities for service, we can help every person who cares to live "the good life."

New York, New York   Alice Korngold
March 2005

Acknowledgments

Building services to engage businesses in strengthening nonprofits has been an extraordinary journey. I work with colleagues throughout the United States to leverage the good will of businesses and their employees of all ages, from all walks of life, in productive and meaningful community involvement. My work is a thrill because I am in daily contact with people who want to make a productive contribution as volunteers. I also have the privilege of working with the men and women who serve as chief executives of nonprofit organizations. Immersed in their fields in health and human services, education, cultural arts, environmental protection, and civic and economic development, they devote their lives to service, and they are the most inspiring, creative, and generous individuals one can ever have the privilege to work with.

My partners are Denise O'Brien and Elizabeth Voudouris. Together, we have created unique and innovative programs to engage people in what we call "high-impact service." I treasure their creative talent, dedication, friendship, and humor.

Thank you to the outstanding team of people who helped me develop and implement services to help nonprofits leverage good will. They include Sigrid Belli, Nicole Clayborne, Barbara Dudas, Tammy Gregg, Jeff Griffiths, Azadeh Hardiman, Kerianne Hearns, Mary Hirsh, Stephanie Johnston, Ann Kent, Shannon McDaniel, Melanie Meyer, and Kathryn Vana.

Thank you to those who "got it" first. They include John M. Bridgeland, Anita Cosgrove, Susan Danilow, Elan Garonzik, Cynthia M. Gibson, Vartan Gregorian, Kathy Lacey, Monica Langley, Kristin Mannion, Richard W. Pogue, Geri M. Presti, Donna M. Sciarappa, and Deborah Vesy.

Most important, thank you to my family, who give me sheer joy and purpose in life. Ethan, my oldest, and his wife, Elena, are physicians in Boston. David is a college student in Massachusetts. All three have vast interests in the arts, politics, and popular culture; life with them is full of learning and humor. And my new grandson, Gabriel, is pure sunshine. My husband, Gerry, has empowered me to become who I am.

Thank you to my editor, Dorothy Hearst, for appreciating the value of this book from our first conversation and for her guidance in shaping the focus. Thank you to Allison Brunner for her assistance. Thank you to Gerry for encouraging me to write this book, and to David and Gerry and Elizabeth Voudouris for their devoted assistance in editing it.

So I circle back to my work and the focus of this book. Life has meaning when we can share our love and good will with others and, yes, help to make this world a better place for our children and grandchildren. I hope that everyone can find and release the power of good will within themselves.

—A. K.

The Author

ALICE KORNGOLD is a national consultant who has assisted hundreds of businesses—including Fortune 500 corporations and leading professional services firms—and nonprofit institutions. Until February 2005, Alice was the president and chief executive officer and in 1993 was the founding chief executive of Business Volunteers Unlimited (BVU). Under Alice's leadership, BVU placed and trained over one thousand business executives and professionals on close to three hundred nonprofit boards of directors. Alice and her work at BVU were featured in a page one article in the *Wall Street Journal* and in other national media. Previously, Alice had developed the Health Trustee Institute for hospital governing boards in Northeast Ohio and, before that, the cooperative-education program on the three campuses of Pace University in New York. Alice was recognized by the *Nonprofit Times* as one of the Power and Influence Top 50 in 2000, 2001, 2003, and 2004. She has a B.A. cum laude and an M.S.Ed. from the University of Pennsylvania. She resides in New York City.

Leveraging
Good Will

Give me a lever long enough and a place
to stand, and I will change the world.

—Archimedes, 230 BCE

1

Why Should Nonprofits Engage with Businesses?

God, grant me work until my life is over, and life until my work is done.
> —Peter Gomes, from a speech to
> a Harvard graduating class, 2004

The phone cried out in my office on a hot summer afternoon in 2000. Ed Bell, board chair of Providence House in Cleveland, Ohio, was on the other end of the line. His organization was in distress, and he did not know what to do about the problems: in addition to the executive director's recent diagnosis of cancer, the organization was facing budget deficits, staffing concerns, board issues, and the impending departure from town of its highly active celebrity fundraiser, without whose support the organization might find itself in a financial crisis. In general, Providence House had immediate problems with day-to-day funding and staffing, and the long-term picture looked dismal.

Five thousand infants and children at risk of neglect and abuse had come to Providence House for help for over twenty years. Housing twenty-six children at a time for up to sixty days at its two residential sites, the organization was open twenty-four hours a day, every day of the year. It was a wonderful organization doing important and noble work, but it would not be able to continue without significant help. Ed asked me to facilitate a discussion with the board. I met with the board members and identified the problems. They needed help in a variety of fields.

At the same time, my staff had interviewed businesspeople who wanted to help an organization just like Providence House: many strategic-planning experts from National City Bank who had experience in fundraising for nonprofits; Paul O'Connor, a senior executive from McDonald Financial Group with a background in strategic planning, marketing, and consulting to small businesses; Frank Zombek, a seasoned professional in human resource development, organizational structures, executive search, and executive compensation; Shelly Walk, an attorney whose expertise ranged from corporate governance to crisis management, strategic planning, and media relations; Denise Dinnie, an accountant from a large national firm; Scott Durham, a successful small-business owner who knew what it meant to juggle many roles and tasks; Terrance Donley, the owner of a major construction company; Veronica Runcis, a corporate-contributions executive from Eaton Corporation; and Eileen Sheil, a public-relations executive who had worked with organizations of various sizes. Each of these individuals had expressed a particular interest in assisting an organization that served young children, and each sought an organization in distress where they could make a meaningful contribution. They had graduate business degrees, law degrees, and years and years of work experience in a wide variety of businesses. Once I helped the Providence House board members identify exactly where they needed help, I put Ed and his fellow board members in touch with this wealth of business talent to make the match. The organization also needed a new executive director. By the end of 2001, the board had appointed Natalie Leek-Nelson to head the organization. She brought fifteen years of nonprofit and corporate experience in education, management, marketing, and program development.

The right people and talents were in place, but the organization needed a catalyst for improvement. I worked with all parties to transfer the skills of the individuals into the nonprofit world. Together, we created board-member standards and expectations, organized the board into functioning committees, focused the board and its agenda on Providence House's key issues, and worked to establish a functioning revenue model to which each board member would contribute.

We developed the board and executive leadership as well. One of the candidates who had been referred by my staff rose to the role of board chair—Paul O'Connor, senior vice president, area banking executive, McDonald Financial Group. By fostering a close working relationship between the successive board chairs and Natalie and teaching them how to bring together the skills of other board members, we made the organization more robust and secure than it had been. Natalie and the board also developed succession plans and used board composition to ensure the health of Providence House for years to come.

Finally, under Paul and Natalie's leadership, Providence House developed a strategic plan to guide the organization in the future. The plan calls for service expansion in residential care, education, counseling, foster care, and noncritical medical care, and for collaborations with other agencies. The plan also calls for the development of additional funding resources.

Once an organization on the brink of collapse, Providence House is now stronger than ever. Since the summer day when the phone rang out in my office, Providence House has almost doubled its revenue to $1.5 million, secured executive and board leadership, assembled a team of board members with crucial skills, and planned for the future. Providence House faces new and daunting financial challenges, but it is well equipped with dedicated board members who will make strategic decisions to serve the organization's mission to serve young children in crisis. Natalie refers to my team members as "the silent partners that help us care for the babies and children of Providence House" (e-mail message, June 2004).

The Challenges Nonprofits Face

Nonprofit organizations profoundly affect the daily lives of all Americans. Nonprofits educate children and adults, cure diseases, care for seniors, treat people who are drug- and alcohol-addicted, train and place people in jobs, and provide day care for children while their parents work. Citizens of all ages enjoy public parks, zoos, museums, and concerts. Communities, families, and citizens thrive or whither depending on the quality and scope of health and human services, education, cultural offerings, and civic and economic development. Yet nonprofits face a new set of challenges today. Constricted and more focused funding, demands for demonstrations of community relevance, and an emphasis on accountability have all created a difficult obstacle course for nonprofits. Although many of these obstacles may be familiar to members of the corporate world, they present unique problems for nonprofits that are not experienced with such issues.

Although the nonprofit sector is vast and its services are essential to daily life, many of these services are provided by a web of relatively small organizations. The financial strain on small and mid-size nonprofits is intense. It is daunting for them to generate resources while juggling to provide day-to-day services. Lester Salamon and Richard O'Sullivan, summarizing the results of a national survey of nonprofits (children and family services, elderly services and housing, community and economic development, museums, and theaters), conclude, "Nearly 90 percent of surveyed organizations reported some level of fiscal stress over the past year, with over half (51 percent) reporting severe or very severe stress" (Salamon and O'Sullivan, 2004, p. 1). These are difficult times for nonprofits.

Not only are nonprofits competing for dollars, but these organizations are also forced to adapt to drastically changing funding patterns. Corporations, community foundations, private philan-thropies, and local, state, and federal governments are changing their funding approaches and expectations. As a result, nonprofits are being challenged to realign their fundraising strategies, organizational structures, and program-delivery models.

Federal and state legislation and government funding patterns have changed the means and purposes for which nonprofits can access dollars. For example, since the mid-1990s, government funding as well as managed-care contracts have favored providers that offer a full spectrum of mental and physical health services to patients of all ages. Although this approach may improve quality and efficiency, it drives nonprofits to establish continuum-of-care collaborations. Creating strategic alliances among a wide variety of providers is highly complex, and nonprofits rarely have the resources to hire the consultants, facilitators, research analysts, and other professionals who are needed to facilitate this change. Consequently, many nonprofits simply struggle with reduced resources, focusing on the day-to-day challenges without the capacity to make the larger leap forward. This situation leads to a highly dysfunctional service system that spirals into increased misery for the staffs of nonprofit organizations and, consequently, weakened services for the community.

As described in a statewide study of the financial health of the nonprofit sector in Illinois (*Illinois Nonprofits*, 1998), nonprofits face serious threats. "Major public policy shifts in government programs have created the double-edged effect of creating greater demand for the services of nonprofits while at the same time reducing the level of public support to carry out such efforts. Examples of such policy shifts include welfare reform, devolution, and managed care. This has resulted in a shortage of income to meet expenses, potentially creating a precarious operating environment for nonprofits" (p. 7).

Furthermore, board members, who rarely have expertise regarding complex nonprofit revenue sources, are confused and critical of what appears on the surface to be a lack of ability on the part of the organization. According to Donna Sciarappa, lead managing director, American Express Tax and Business Services in northern Ohio, "Many nonprofit organizations have highly complex revenue structures that are not at all familiar to businesspeople. A single organization with an annual operating budget of $30 million can have more than twenty different funding sources, each with very different requirements regarding billing, timing, eligibility, and reporting. Without the background or training, boards would not understand the general ledger and the subsidiary ledgers. You are asking volunteer board members to understand a very different line of business. Compare this to the for-profit sector, where many businesses have one single source of revenue—customers who make purchases" (interview, April 23, 2004).

Governments are not the only revenue source that has changed the rules. Corporations have also altered their giving priorities, further adding to the challenges of nonprofits in generating funding. Corporations are becoming increasingly strategic, focusing their donations in particular areas that complement their business missions. For example, some banks are zeroing in on workforce development because, as financial institutions, they recognize that their success is intertwined with that of the community. Through workforce development, a bank can help create employees and customers for the future, while also strengthening the overall economic health of its community. Although it is laudable that businesses are investing in nonprofit services that will yield economic development for the community, the changes in funding priorities bring new pressures to organizations; many are left out altogether if their services are not aligned with the funder's priorities.

Community foundations, private philanthropies, and individuals are also reorienting their focus and attention. They too are seeking to more clearly define their areas of interest to achieve greater impact. For example, the Edna McConnell Clark Foundation focuses on youth development with a particular emphasis on strategic planning and board development. At the regional level, many foundations are pooling their funds specifically for economic development with a focus on entrepreneurship and innovation. Understandably, funders are looking at the most pressing national and regional community interests and seeking to allocate finite resources where they will have the most meaningful impact. For example, many foundations are sending the message to cultural-arts organizations that funding will be focused on programs that expose urban children to musical, visual, and performance arts and that provide classes in them. Foundations tend to value programs that fill gaps in public school education and also provide a way to develop the next generation of cultural consumers.

Although these newer foundation strategies may be worthy approaches that will bring positive results for communities, the new funding priorities put extraordinary demands on nonprofits that have been relying on certain funding sources and patterns in order to provide vital community services. Many of the organizations with diminished support continue on in a cycle of organizational misery or discontinue programs that clearly provide value to key elements of society. However, some of these nonprofits are merging into other organizations that are healthier financially, to the benefit of the community.

We are also witnessing the dawn of heightened accountability, which has particular implications for the nonprofit sector. Funders are placing new demands on nonprofits to measure and document their impact in addressing social, cultural, economic, and education issues. For-profit companies have to show their financial results, including return on investment, on a regular basis; likewise, nonprofits are now expected to show return on investment in the sense of achieving positive results for the benefit of the community.

Although accountability is good, the task of measuring outcomes can be daunting for many organizations that lack the experience, expertise, and resources to create and establish measurement systems. Furthermore, it is exceedingly more difficult for a nonprofit to show that it is achieving its mission than it is for a for-profit, which needs simply to document monetary profits. For many nonprofits, measurement is quite elusive, especially when the outcomes of services are long-term and involve a variety of factors. For example, organizations that provide arts programs for inner-city children are being asked to demonstrate that their programs facilitate the long-term educational and career success of the children who participate. Such longitudinal studies are expensive, and it is difficult to tease out the value of a particular service such as one arts-education program. According to Jan Masaoka, executive director of CompassPoint Nonprofit Services in San Francisco, "Effectiveness is difficult to measure partly because social causes and effects are difficult to measure, but also because the long-term and broad goals of an organization are hard for any one funder to commit to" (Masaoka, 2003, pp. 82–83). Thus, boards, funders, and the public that support nonprofits need to be reasonable in their expectations surrounding measurement.

Furthermore, measurements can distract the nonprofit organization from its mission by encouraging the wrong behaviors. For example, if a welfare-to-work training program measures the number of people who complete training and are placed in jobs, then the staff will be encouraged to ramp up the rate of placements rather than providing other forms of support, such as counseling and follow-up services, that would better ensure the long-term success of the clients. Schools that seek to increase passing scores on standardized state exams may focus exclusively on training children to take tests, at the expense of exciting children about learning so they will stay in school longer.

Nonprofits are thus performing a high-wire act: at the same time they are providing services, new challenges force them to create entirely new ways of accessing funds and delivering services. These strategic and financial challenges require time and resources, and they also need organizational muscles and skill sets that have not traditionally been exercised to a great extent by nonprofit executives and boards. Nonprofits are known for their commitment to mission and service, they often perform mightily in the face of distress, and they are certainly adept at stretching limited resources. In this new era, however, nonprofits can succeed only by applying dynamic and aggressive business strategies. With innovative organizational structures and methods, nonprofits can improve their results, and these results in turn generate the increased support that allows them to rise to new levels of performance.

The Need for Business Expertise in the Nonprofit Sector

Given this entirely new landscape of challenges in funding, relevance, and accountability, the nonprofit sector needs to explore new ways of doing business. Nonprofits are already beginning to reconsider their missions and visions by assessing community needs, evaluating and reestablishing their relevance, focusing their programs and services for the greatest possible impact, measuring and documenting their effectiveness, and, most significantly, redesigning their financial models to support their programs and services. In order to survive, nonprofits that make it will be those that re-create themselves.

Reinvention of this magnitude requires expertise in strategic and financial planning, mergers and affiliations, pricing, communications, market research, negotiations, human resource management and development, information technology, and facilities planning. The advanced skill sets required in the nonprofit sector thus mirror those skills that are required in for-profit businesses.

A high-functioning governance model and an outstanding chief executive are key requisites for successfully channeling corporate know-how to address the strategic issues facing nonprofits and to take organizations to a new level of effectiveness. Unfortunately, nonprofit boards have not traditionally been expected to perform in the manner that is required in this new and demanding environment. Expectations of individual board members and the board as a whole have been random and lax. Notions of board members bringing "wealth, wisdom, or work" to the board table are usually defined in loose terms with no serious accountability. In many cases, because there has been so little clarity, board members think they are being useful even when they are not.

Furthermore, the executives who run nonprofits have sometimes risen through the ranks of direct service without training or experience in developing or running complex enterprises. Outstanding social workers may have a solid understanding of the field of service and even the community's needs; however, they may have little background in organizational leadership and development. As chief executives, they need to generate significant revenues, establish a staffing structure to maximize program outcomes, create measurement systems to demonstrate organizational relevance and success, and possibly negotiate strategic alliances with other organizations. Without these executive skills, the organization faces a rocky road in the new, dynamic environment. The salary structure for chief executives themselves is entirely inadequate in today's world as well. Furthermore, the chief executive of a nonprofit rarely has the resources needed to hire, as an important member of the senior team, a financial officer of the caliber routinely hired in for-profit businesses.

Businesses Want to Help

At the same time that nonprofits are seeking to adopt businesslike practices to advance their causes, businesses and their employees are seeking increased volunteer involvement in the community. The timing of these two trends presents an extraordinary opportunity for nonprofits to access the business expertise they need on a volunteer basis. Business volunteers can make a powerful contribution to nonprofits by serving as volunteer management consultants and as board members. As Mary Egan of the Boston Consulting Group in New York City observes, "Businesspeople can help nonprofit boards with activities that are core to most large, successful business—for example, forecasting or strategic planning. Many of the 'growing pains' experienced by social entrepreneurs mirror those experienced by entrepreneurs in the for-profit sector. Many of the learnings are applicable across both groups" (interview, January 24, 2005).

Leveraging Good Will

Given the interest of volunteers in providing meaningful and productive volunteer service, this is the time for nonprofits to leverage good will. A lever is a tool to convert an input of a small amount of force or energy into a far greater output. By engaging a single volunteer who can contribute just the right expertise to a nonprofit, an organization can leverage the small input to make stunning changes that improve its ability to thrive.

A seesaw is a lever. A small child using a simple playground seesaw as a lever can lift an adult three feet off the ground, a feat that could not be achieved with the child's own arms. Likewise, one volunteer, with the right skills and a reasonable commitment of time, can bring about tremendous outcomes by strengthening a nonprofit. Imagine thousands of volunteers involved with organizations that need their expertise. The impact could be transformative for the nation's nonprofit sector.

For example, a law professor who has a doctorate in economics in addition to a law degree joined a nonprofit that reached out to rural women in need of drug- and alcohol-treatment services; when he joined the board, the nonprofit was rapidly heading toward closure because of financial distress. Within four months, this new board member led the organization in merging into a larger nonprofit and establishing long-term funding support for the programs from four local foundations. This board member was not a wealthy individual with a big bankroll; instead, he offered business acumen and a commitment to ensuring the viability of vital community services. His work over the critical four-month period took about fifty hours. That is leverage.

The case of a partner at a national consulting firm provides another example of leverage. An expert in pricing, his analysis and advice saved a regional nonprofit from a downward spiral of financial deficits by helping the organization realign its financial model. This is leverage: using a small amount of energy—time and expertise, in this case—to yield a larger result.

In order for nonprofits to achieve this leverage, they need to articulate the challenges they face, consider the new heights they seek to achieve, identify the skills and expertise that can be most useful, and then pursue suitable matches with volunteer personnel. Nonprofits that figure out what they need can reach out to new volunteers who can help evaluate community needs, assess the need for services, identify funding opportunities, and figure out optimal organizational structures and strategic alliances. The ultimate goal is to generate support for quality programs and services that meet vital community needs.

According to David G. Poplack, M.D., Director of Texas Children's Cancer Center, in Houston, Texas, who serves on numerous nonprofit boards, "Business people who serve on nonprofit boards help to focus the organization on its key strategic issues, articulate clear plans to achieve overarching goals, and establish realistic financial structures to support the nonprofit and its core programs and services" (interview, January 24, 2005).

Business Volunteers and Matchmakers

Business volunteers are volunteers with business skills. Business volunteers are not exclusively from the for-profit sector. Many of the most effective volunteers come from academia, health care institutions, and other nonprofit and governmental agencies. As will be established in Chapter Two, these business volunteers and their employers provide benefits by developing organizations' leadership, enhancing their reputations, and helping to build strong communities.

Matchmakers are community organizations—themselves nonprofits—that can serve as the conduit between nonprofits and businesses. Skilled and trained matchmakers can be highly useful to non-profits in assessing their needs for business assistance, engaging businesses and their personnel in volunteer service and preparing them for such service, and ensuring effective matches between talented volunteers and nonprofits that need them. Consider the matchmaker as the fulcrum that rests under the middle of the lever (again, imagine a seesaw); the fulcrum can help both sides benefit—in this case, the nonprofit and the volunteer (and even the volunteer's sponsor, her or his employer). Both parties can be raised to a new level: the nonprofit to greater effectiveness and the volunteer to greater satisfaction, stronger leadership, and improved networking. Chapter Three addresses the role of the matchmaker in depth.

Selecting Board Members

Traditional approaches for selecting and engaging board members and nonprofit executives will not suffice in today's complex economic and social environment. In this new era, nonprofit executives and board members need to be selected based on their qualifications and expertise in organizational, financial, and strategic development. For example, an organization that has run a financial deficit for three years and that has drained its cash reserves and endowment funds needs people with business skills to help develop a new financial model and business plan; all programs and services need to be put on the table alongside an evaluation of potential revenue sources in order to create an organizational plan that is financially sustainable. This plan may even involve a new strategic alliance or merger with an organization that can ensure the viability of the most essential services.

Another problem is that so many nonprofits have had to adapt to funding changes by making a series of incremental adjustments according to the ebbs and flows of available money and the interests of various funders. Unfortunately, step-by-step changes over two or three years, absent a larger organizational plan, leave an organization without an effective working model. Deborah Vesy, executive director of the Deaconess Community Foundation in Lorain, Ohio, points out that "there comes a point when the board and chief executive need to take a big step back and rethink the entire structure and redesign the organization accordingly" (interview, December 8, 2004). In other words, step-by-step changes work only when an organization has a broader vision.

In order to lead organizations in rethinking their structures and services, nonprofit boards of directors must comprise people who are experienced in strategy, finance, accounting, investments, public relations, marketing, advocacy, organizational development, human resources, law, real estate, information technology, facilities planning, construction, and other business arenas. G. Kennedy Thompson, chairman and chief executive officer (CEO) of Wachovia Corporation, observes that "the strategic realignments that nonprofits are having to make are similar to those that are made in the for-profit sector. Businesspeople are used to having to adapt to changes in the marketplace; their experience can be useful to nonprofits having to be sufficiently nimble to adjust to funding challenges as well as calls for relevance and accountability" (interview, April 13, 2004). Thompson also cautions that nonprofits must be clear about their missions and stay true to their purposes while they adapt their strategies according to new demands and expectations of funders and the community.

In addition, the chief executives of nonprofits must have experience in leading organizations, and they need to have firm control of the helm. As pointed out by Michael Marn, a partner at McKinsey & Co. in Cleveland, Ohio, "The burden of organizational success is more concentrated in the chief executive of a nonprofit than a for-profit in that she will not have the resources to hire a senior team with the financial, strategic, and human resources expertise. In order to be effective, the chief executive of the nonprofit has to be outstanding in all areas of executive management, and it is the rare person who has such strength in every arena" (interview, April 29, 2004). Thus, nonprofits require particularly outstanding chief executives who have the range and depth of ability to lead, and the most effective nonprofit executives are the ones who know how to draw on the business acumen that resides in the board.

Although the board has a fiduciary oversight role, and board members can contribute invaluable expertise, it is the organization's CEO who is immersed in the nonprofit sector, the funding environment, and the work of the organization. CEOs are the ultimate experts; they devote themselves more than full time to the work of nonprofits, and they need to lead their organizations in articulating missions, developing and implementing an organizational plan, providing measurable outcomes, and generating support.

Organizations that understand the new funding, relevance, and accountability challenges are beginning to strengthen governance by rebuilding their boards and to enhance organizational effectiveness by hiring highly qualified chief executives. Change is possible and has happened in many organizations. The first step is for the nonprofit to assess itself and what it needs in order to achieve increased support and effectiveness.

Assessing Your Organization: What Help Do You Need?

Businesses are interested in helping nonprofits, but the organizations themselves must first figure out what help will be most useful. According to Shannon W. McFayden, senior executive vice president and director of corporate and community affairs at Wachovia Corporation, "We are committed to involving our executives in helping nonprofit organizations. When nonprofit organizations that contact us for board members are clear about what they need in terms of expertise, we can be more helpful by suggesting the right candidates from among our many executives" (interview, April 13, 2004). Thus, organizations that clearly describe the volunteer assistance they need are in the best position to capitalize on the availability of business volunteers. Input from a variety of organizational stakeholders is useful in conducting an organizational assessment. Perspectives that can be helpful come from foundations, businesses, volunteers, board members, staff members, donors, clients, and others who are involved with the community and the issues that are addressed by the organization.

At a roundtable discussion among eight nonprofit executives in Chicago at the INDEPENDENT SECTOR annual national conference in 2004, the executives asked how to find businesspeople who could help their organizations. The head of an urban arts organization asked how he could appeal to business executives who could lend professional expertise to help his organization with its revenue model. Similar concerns were raised by the executive of a social service organization that promotes wellness and fitness for women and the head of an early-childhood-intervention program. A nonprofit in Los Angeles inquired about linking with businesses that have an interest in organizations that promote educational opportunities for minority individuals.

Listed below are a few key areas where businesspeople can add perspective to nonprofit boards. By reviewing this list, nonprofits can determine where they need help and then identify and recruit individuals with suitable backgrounds.

Mission

First and foremost, an organization needs to take a fresh and critical look at its mission—the organization's purpose—in order to ensure that the organization is relevant in today's environment. In revisiting its mission, the organization should focus on the needs of the community. This external analysis should involve demographic research as well as surveys, interviews, focus groups, and data from academic or research institutions. Based on the research, the organization can determine the scope of the need, the compelling value of services that can be offered by the organization, and the level of potential support for the cause.

Businesspeople with expertise in market research, strategic analysis, visioning, and group process can be useful in assessing mission. People with a variety of backgrounds and perspectives can broaden the organization's concept of itself and suggest how it can provide compelling value to diverse constituencies.

Vision

The organization also needs to develop a view of what it will become in order to provide the greatest value in the most effective manner. A vision statement describes the optimal future of a nonprofit. Here again, people from business who have shown creativity and vision can help, as can individuals with a range of backgrounds from a variety of communities.

Programs and Services

After revisiting the mission and affirming or adjusting it accordingly and after setting a vision, the organization is set to review the key programs and services that will have the greatest impact in achieving the mission and vision. In order to focus organizational resources for the greatest value, it might be necessary to add new and innovative programs that have proven successful elsewhere, eliminate obsolete or less effective programs, or collaborate with other organizations. It is important to research how other communities are addressing similar needs and to adopt best practices that are demonstrating results; other communities can also provide insights about practices, programs, or services that are not effective.

People with experience in organizational development, human resources, benchmarking (assessing effectiveness, efficiencies, and results based on comparative data of like organizations), strategic consulting, and finance can be useful as an organization considers the relative value, impact, effectiveness, and sustainability of its various programs; diverse backgrounds and knowledge of the community are essential in order to avoid myopia.

Organizational Capacity

An internal assessment should focus on the organization's capacities and capabilities to provide the services that are needed. The organization should consider strengths and weaknesses in the quality and scope of programs and services presently offered; the CEO's qualifications, performance, and commitment; the staff's experience and qualifications; financial resources, relationships with funders, and fundraising expertise; the adequacy of the organization's information systems and the resources that would be required to upgrade them as needed; and the level of the board members' expertise, relationships, diversity, commitment, and engagement.

Fundraising, philanthropy, foundation relations, public relations, marketing, communications, human resources, endowments, law, government relations, contracting, finance, accounting, and sometimes real estate are just a few of the business skill sets that will be useful.

The Financial Model and Revenue Structure

An organization's viability depends on its having a solid financial model. In today's environment, improving an organization's financial situation often means narrowing down priority programs and then revising the revenue model. It is useful for organizations to examine each key revenue source and the likelihood of its continuing in the future. Weak sources need to be replaced, and new sources need to be explored and cultivated. By identifying those who care most about the organization, the nonprofit can develop a compelling case, tailoring it to particular interests. For example, the county might be interested in an organization moving single mothers from welfare to work through training and placement services, while a private foundation might be particularly focused on quality day care for the children of the mothers who work. Given a variety of funding sources and their particular interests, the nonprofit can build a revenue model that supports the entire enterprise. Here again, individuals with business expertise and perspectives and with diverse backgrounds and experiences will be critical for success.

The organization also needs to explore ways to access new funding sources, perhaps by researching federal grants, arranging personal introductions to wealthy individuals, holding meetings with and or otherwise gaining access to local county councilpersons, or combining these approaches. The nonprofit needs to identify the expertise, experience, and relationships that will be necessary in order to access funds and then determine whether the expertise and relationships are available from staff members, volunteer consultants, paid consultants, board members, or a combination of these resources.

Organizations are often tempted to eliminate services that are the greatest financial burden. However, those may well be the most mission-related programs, especially insofar as they serve the neediest populations. In creating a revenue model, organizations need to look at the entire funding picture; it may be possible to cross-subsidize in order to support some of the most critical services. For example, an art museum might find support for its high-profile traveling exhibits from wealthy patrons, corporations, and established foundations; at the same time, surpluses from sponsorships and ticket fees might provide critical funding for programs for children who are deprived of access to art education. At the end of the day, funds from a variety of sources need to fully support the mix of programs and services that are most valuable in addressing community concerns.

Measurement

By measuring, documenting, and reporting on the value and impact of their programs and services, nonprofits gain information for planning, while also strengthening their case for support. The chief executive, with board input, needs to clearly define the ways in which the organization seeks to have an impact, in accordance with the mission, and then determine ways to quantify the extent to which the nonprofit is making a difference. For example, food banks should evaluate and report on pounds of food collected and distributed, numbers of meals served, and numbers of people fed. Museums should monitor and publicize numbers of visitors as well as numbers of participants in classes, including demographic distributions to show the extent to which they reach people of all ages and from every segment of the community. Drug- and alcohol-treatment services should study and show how many people are treated as well as the longer-term results for people in recovery. Results should be tied back to costs of services to show the impact based on the money raised. Donors are more likely to increase their gifts if they can see how their contributions are used. Businesspeople can lend their acumen in helping nonprofits to capture information that will demonstrate the compelling value of their programs. People who are expert in communications can be particularly helpful in thinking about the information that needs to be evaluated and relayed and in what fashion in order to galvanize support.

Collaboration Among Organizations

An organization should take a candid look at other organizations that meet similar or related community needs. There might be opportunities to align with these organizations, thereby enhancing the services, the case for funding, and organizational efficiencies. Nonprofit organizations should examine for-profit, nonprofit, and government agencies. Some potential partners can offer an array of services that are vertical, meaning that they provide a "cradle-to-grave" spectrum of programs that help clients with a variety of related issues. For example, a workforce training program might provide job training, job placement, day care, financial counseling, legal assistance, and job-retention assistance. Other organizations that are potential collaborators can offer horizontal services, meaning that they focus on one service. An example of a horizontal service is a food center that collects, warehouses, and distributes food to soup kitchens that serve the hungry in all corners of the community. In looking at other service providers, a nonprofit should consider the characteristics that make each of them desirable or not desirable as a partner.

The Value Businesses Bring . . . and the Caveats

Business skills are highly useful tools for an organization to use to assess itself and to develop a vision and plan given the current environment. At the same time, companies have begun to realize that their businesses depend on healthy economies in the communities where their employees live and work. In addition, businesses understand that their employees prefer and appreciate employers that invest in their communities. Businesses recognize that volunteer service enhances the personal, professional, and leadership development of their employees. Finally, companies see the opportunity to build good will and develop public relations. Thus, through volunteerism, businesses can leverage their assistance to nonprofits in order to improve their own positions in the community. According to Tiffany L. Rowe, director, strategic planning, Washington Hospital Healthcare System, in Fremont, California, "the most forward-thinking companies understand that encouraging their employees to lead authentic, meaningful lives results in a better-balanced and productive team. But actively assisting an employee to find a passion outside of the workplace takes that commitment a step further and will ultimately promote a professional culture that celebrates diversity of perspective and experience" (interview, January 24, 2005).

Until recently, the predominant focus of business volunteering was on "done-in-a-day" projects. These large-scale, one-day events engage hundreds or thousands of businesspeople and their families and often generate public acclaim for the participating companies. These days of service can be productive for cleaning up playgrounds and cemeteries, painting shelters and schools, serving hot meals to the homeless, or distributing school supplies to children. These volunteer programs are a wonderful way to mobilize large groups of people and to generate public enthusiasm for volunteering. An added benefit is that some employees continue volunteering at the host site long after the done-in-a-day is over. Beyond conducting days of service, many businesses also encourage and support employees who tutor and mentor children and perform other longer-term volunteer activities. According to studies conducted by the Independent Sector, people who volunteer are more likely to make personal financial contributions to the organization and to give more than nonvolunteers.

Although these direct volunteer services are important, they represent only one way that companies can help strengthen communities. Today, there is an extraordinary opportunity to involve talented people from businesses, academia, government services, and other nonprofits in high-impact service through nonprofit board involvement and volunteer management assistance. Given corporate interests in productive community involvement, nonprofits can attract the experience and expertise that they need to address critical strategic and financial challenges. There are risks, however, in involving businesspeople in decision making in the nonprofit sector: businesspeople need to learn how to make the translation to the nonprofit environment. They need to understand the fundamental difference between a mission-driven approach and a profit-driven approach. For example, a businessperson might be inclined to cut a program or service that is not financially sustainable, but that may be the service that provides the most necessary services to those in the greatest need. In addition, businesspeople need to learn how to engage in the nonprofit decision-making process, which is different from decision making in the corporate culture.

Using Business Volunteers to Enhance Multiculturalism and Dialogue

Nonprofit organizations are magnets for people from diverse backgrounds. Nonprofits provide the common ground for rallying around mutual interests that vary from breast cancer, to performing arts, to hospice care, to mentoring, to higher education. Nonprofits that build on this opportunity to reach out to a variety of communities have a great advantage in that they deepen their value and provide a learning environment for all who participate.

Additionally, the nation's citizens can increase their understanding of important social and political matters by volunteering in communities with which they are not familiar. One example is that of an attorney who joined the board of an organization that helps Latino immigrants develop language skills and obtain jobs in their new country. The board candidate would not have even been aware of this organization had the matchmaker not suggested it in the course of an interview. Through the attorney's new involvement on this organization's board, he reconnected with his own family history; his forebears had been immigrants from Macedonia a few generations earlier. Through his volunteer service, he recognized his common bond with newcomers and developed his understanding of the challenges facing them. Another example is that of an investment banker who joined the board of a domestic-violence center. He broke a barrier by being the first man on the board and became a valued member, raising questions and providing perspectives that enriched board discussions.

An organization that facilitates the hiring of women (many of whom are single mothers) in well-paying, skilled, union jobs in the trades provides another example. The board is a mix of trades-women and middle-class professionals. A new member of the board, a consultant with a national firm, has added immense value by documenting and communicating the economic case for this organization. This board member condensed hundreds of files to show how much income the women earn once they go through the organization's program ($60,000 a year for life); how many homes have been bought by these women once they get jobs in the trades; how much they are contributing in taxes; how much welfare funding is saved; how many women and children gain access to health care through their new union jobs; and how attractive it is to employers to have access to a ready pool of trained workers. With these key data boiled down to a few points, the organization is positioned to access deep pockets of funding that have been set aside for economic development. The organization, with an annual budget of $500,000, can now show that if it had a budget of a few million dollars, the local economy would be strengthened. In these cases, the businessperson adds value, and the board provides a learning environment. Together, their common bond is their commitment to the organization and its mission.

Nonprofit boards that include people from a broad variety of communities and backgrounds are stronger strategically. People who serve on boards are in turn personally enriched by engaging in decision making with people who have differing perspectives. And the community is stronger when it is led by people with a rich variety of experiences.

Engaging the Next Generation

Now is a particularly auspicious time to engage volunteers in strengthening the nonprofit sector through board service and volunteer management assistance. With the emergence of the "Millennial generation," born in and after 1982 and graduating from high school in 2000 and later, the nation is seeing the dawn of a service renaissance. This generation has an extraordinary level of engagement in community service. The Millennials have been involved in volunteerism through their schools, and they show evidence of continuing their interest as they grow. Studies conducted by Neil Howe and William Strauss indicate that the Millennial generation has been raised to appreciate the importance of service.

> By the Millennial era, the notion of volunteering gave way to a more compulsory "service learning," which is now often required for graduation from middle or high

school. Bolstered by Acts of Congress in 1990 and 1993, which created the Learn and Serve America program, the integration of community service with academic study has spread to schools everywhere. From 1984 to 1999, the share of high schools offering any kind of community service program grew from 27 to 83 percent, and the share with "service learning" grew from 9 to 46 percent. Two-thirds of all public schools at all grade levels now have students engaged in community work, often as a part of the curriculum.

A new Millennial service ethic is emerging, built around notions of collegial (rather than individual) action, support for (rather than resistance against) civic institutions, the tangible doing of good deeds [Howe and Strauss, 2000, p. 216].

According to Peter Gomes, chaplain at Harvard University, the Millennials are unique in their interest in seeking what he calls "the good life," including service to the community. "In this generation the search for goodness, both institutional and personal, has reappeared as a defining characteristic in young people's renewed search for the good life. . . . The fundamental question of the young . . . is, simply, 'what will it take for me to make a good life, and not merely a good living?'" (Gomes, 2002, p. 23).

As Millennials move into the job market, employers are already seeing evidence of their interest in service and the community. Managing partners of many professional-services firms are establishing and expanding their volunteer programs in order to attract and retain the most highly qualified new graduates. Furthermore, many of these graduates have taken newly created college and graduate school courses in nonprofit governance and management with the intention of becoming involved in service to their communities. As the best-educated generation in this nation's history, and with the support of their employers, Millennials can become a powerful force in contributing their knowledge and passion to strengthening the nonprofit sector.

The Bottom Line

To be successful in this dynamic new environment and to address challenges in funding, relevance, and accountability, nonprofits are moving toward entrepreneurial and businesslike approaches. This development in the nonprofit sector presents an unprecedented opportunity for businesspeople to help nonprofits survive and thrive. Based on the experiences of businesspeople who provide volunteer management assistance and serve on boards, not only do nonprofits benefit, but the volunteers derive extraordinary satisfaction from their service.

As businesses encourage their people to get involved in community service, nonprofits can revitalize themselves by leveraging the good will of businesspeople in order to focus, strengthen, and elevate their organizations. When nonprofits draw on new resources and become increasingly strategic, the community benefits.

2

Why Should Businesses Engage
with Nonprofits?

*The most powerful thing a corporation can do for any
society, or any location in which it operates, is to help
that location create a prosperous economy. If a region
can create a prosperous economy, then it can improve
the standard of living and quality of life of its citizens
for the long term.*
   —Michael E. Porter, Corporate Philanthropy, 2003

Nonprofits that understand why businesses are interested in
becoming involved with them are in the best position to
leverage that good will. Businesses have begun to understand that
philanthropy and volunteerism increase respect for companies
among employees and consumers. As their experiences with their
communities have evolved, businesses are learning how to leverage
their involvement to increase the benefits for the companies themselves, their employees, and their communities. According to the
Center for Corporate Citizenship at Boston College (2003, p. 11),
"Over the years, community relations has moved from the margins
of the corporation to a position of growing importance. More companies regard their involvement in the community as a key business
strategy and a linchpin in their overall citizenship efforts." This
trend among businesses provides fertile ground for nonprofits to engage businesses and their employees in service to the community.

Importantly, businesses are shifting their view about philanthropy and volunteerism. According to Eric Eckholdt, executive director, Credit Suisse First Boston Foundation, New York.

> Our company's approach is evolving. A decade ago, when we became more strategic about giving, we focused on one or two key issues such as education. Today we realize that we can do the most for the community by encouraging and supporting CSFB's employees who volunteer, including those who serve on nonprofit boards and provide volunteer consulting assistance to nonprofits. This brings about several important benefits. First of all, we as a company can have a greater impact in helping the community when we invest our dollars where our people are providing talent and expertise. Additionally, we are fostering the personal, professional, and leadership development of our folks when we support their involvement in service [interview, November 12, 2004].

By understanding what motivates companies to become involved, nonprofit organizations can determine how to engage businesses in the most useful way. In this regard communitywide matchmakers can be used to advantage. Matchmaking services can be based at nonprofit resource centers, volunteer centers, and other nonprofit organizations that are established for the purpose of involving volunteers and strengthening nonprofits. Community foundations and private philanthropies can elevate the nonprofit sector by investing in good matching services. (Matchmaking is discussed further in Chapter Three.)

Understanding Why Businesses Get Involved

Although each business has its own objectives for involvement, generally the six key motivating forces discussed below drive corporate community involvement.

Developing Leadership

For-profit businesses invest tens of millions of dollars in executive leadership development by conducting employee assessments, sponsoring corporate training programs, sending people to national conferences and educational forums, and reimbursing executives and professionals for graduate business programs. Certificate programs at the nation's top business schools thrive on attendance by businesspeople who are sent by their employers. Through a vast education and training industry, businesses have demonstrated their ever-growing commitment to identifying, developing, and grooming younger and more diverse managers and executives for leadership.

Businesses are beginning to recognize that nonprofit-board service presents an important opportunity to develop leadership skills among rising executives. In fact, many businesses, particularly professional-services firms, expect their executives and professionals to serve on boards in order to achieve promotions. People who serve on boards develop new skills by learning how to identify tough organizational challenges, assess strategic options, make the case for certain solutions, build consensus among volunteer board members (tougher than building support among people who work under you), and take responsibility for bringing about constructive changes. Leadership skills such as these are developed by acting under difficult circumstances, not by attending courses.

According to Joel Getz, president, Mayor's Fund to Advance New York, in New York City, "There are pools of talented people who can add immeasurably to nonprofits if they are carefully matched and properly trained. In addition, service on nonprofit boards allows rising leaders, especially younger businesspeople, an opportunity to engage in higher level, strategic decision making—an experience that will help accelerate leadership development for the business environment as well" (interview, January 24, 2005).

Board members who succeed in effecting strategic innovations, forging organizational alliances, leading a fundraising effort, planning an organizational downsizing, or guiding an organization through a troubling media situation rise to challenges that are often more complicated than any business challenge. Business leaders attest that junior executives bring new insights and skills to the workplace once they have exercised the judgment and demonstrated the leadership to facilitate change in the dynamic nonprofit universe.

Michael Marn, a partner at McKinsey & Co. in Cleveland, Ohio, makes this observation about the professionals at his firm and among his clients. "When people join boards, invariably their leadership quotient goes up very quickly. In a typical business situation, you find people similar to you, neck-in-neck, with very similar tool sets. Whereas, the businessperson who joins a board can take his or her skill sets, add value, and stand out. For example, business consultants are trained to listen and learn and then zero in on the key strategic issues. When businesspeople add value in a volunteer board role, they develop confidence and begin emerging as leaders" (interview, April 2004).

Andrea Hunt, vice president of innovation and strategic initiatives at Baxter International in Deerfield, Illinois, comments that "the corporation is a component of the larger community. Through service on regional and national nonprofit boards, we gain a better perspective of society and its multiple constituencies, thereby making us better decision makers in business (interview, January 24, 2005).

Geralyn M. Presti, general counsel, senior vice president, and assistant secretary at Forest City Enterprises in Cleveland, Ohio, also comments on the value of nonprofit-board involvement for rising executives. "In my company's strategic plan, we are developing the future managers, and nonprofit boards provide the venue and opportunity for important leadership development. By performing well in key roles on nonprofit boards, our company's rising stars acquire skills and abilities that will lead to promotion opportunities in the corporate setting" (interview, May 25, 2004).

Facilitating Team Building

In the 1970s and 1980s, outdoor leadership programs became popular among business groups seeking to foster team building among their executives. Businesses believed that the rugged and intense struggle up mountainous terrain and through swift rapids would bond work teams and foster the skills, confidence, and trust necessary to expand the group's productivity. Today, companies recognize the value of volunteering as a team-building exercise. Many businesses have established national and international days of service during which employees build playgrounds, paint homeless shelters, plant gardens at senior centers, and build homes for the poor. Nonprofits such as Habitat for Humanity have learned to access vast volunteer resources to build homes throughout the world. Food banks also provide wonderful volunteer team experiences while benefiting the community by sorting and distributing food to shelters.

Interestingly, roles often shift in the volunteer setting; the employees who emerge as the project leaders are not necessarily the leaders in the business stratum. People with routine and subordinate jobs may show their creativity, initiative, and charisma in leading the group at the volunteer work site. Still others may emerge as the most helpful and supportive of their colleagues in the face of a physical challenge. This experience can establish newfound respect for people who might not normally be noticed for their leadership. Additionally, employers find that after people do a volunteer project together, they become more comfortable calling on each other in the workplace for advice or assistance; the volunteer experience can draw office workers together in a new spirit of camaraderie that is valuable to businesses large and small.

Employees who volunteer together derive a sense of satisfaction from having accomplished a project that is visual, meaningful, and rewarding. After building a playground, volunteers can enjoy the satisfaction of seeing a group of children run to the new equipment with their youthful exuberance and spirit. This positive experience can enhance the employees' view of the employer who encouraged this activity. In the meantime, the children get a new playground! One good day's work, and everybody wins.

Enhancing an Appreciation of Diversity

Smart employers establish workplaces that include talented and qualified people from a variety of backgrounds. By reaching out to the broadest range of people, employers expand the pool of potential employees and thus increase the likelihood of hiring the most talented individuals. Additionally, groups that comprise diverse members are more likely to understand a variety of customers and clients and to be creative in planning and problem solving. Nothing is more stultifying for a business than having a homogeneous group of people trying to serve a heterogeneous group of customers and clients.

Community service provides an advantage by exposing employees to a wide range of people from a variety of cultures and backgrounds. Volunteers who venture into communities different from their own learn about the range and variety of cultures, including rural, urban, artistic, immigrant, and international communities. As we become more and more clustered in homogeneous groupings, volunteering becomes increasingly important in broadening our awareness and understanding of others. Through service, employees develop an appreciation of people who are facing problems different from their own. As we gain new insights regarding diverse communities, we can discuss our experiences at the family table and among friends, thereby spreading our new familiarity with important social and cultural matters. Companies that encourage and support volunteerism help to strengthen our communities and our nation through a better-informed citizenry. Businesses thrive when the cities they inhabit thrive.

According to Robert Axelrod, in *The Evolution of Cooperation*, "Cooperation does occur and . . . our civilization is based upon it. . . . An excellent way to promote cooperation in a society is to teach people to care about the welfare of others" (1984, p. 134). For example, imagine the employees who live and work in an affluent suburb that comprises primarily second- and third-generation Americans. Through volunteer service to a nonprofit organization that assists new immigrants with job and language training, the volunteer may gain increased understanding of the challenges facing society's newest members. Through board service at a center for children with disabilities, a volunteer may come to appreciate the power of motivation in facing adversity. A volunteer who assists every summer at a camp for children with cancer may be inspired by these young people and their zest for life. By providing management assistance to a shelter for abused women and children, a volunteer may expand his or her awareness of a serious and pervasive threat to our society. These volunteer experiences are likely to enrich the volunteers, helping them develop themselves personally and professionally, at the same time that they are providing value to the nonprofit organization.

The educational value of volunteerism spreads even further when volunteers involve their own children in service. Engaging families presents yet another benefit as well. According to INDE-PENDENT SECTOR, children of parents who volunteer are more likely to volunteer themselves as adults. So the benefits of service are exponential. Volunteerism can be leveraged to develop oneself, encourage the next generation, and deepen citizen awareness and understanding of the rich complexities of the United States (*The New Nonprofit Almanac IN BRIEF*, 2001.)

Fostering Loyalty to the Company and a Sense of Community

Employees, as well as their families, friends, and neighbors, can come to understand the full range of people served by nonprofits: people who need day care, health care, services for alcohol and drug recovery, job training and employment, advice for children born with disabilities, assistance with elderly or disabled adults, and counseling and support for mental illness, in addition to everyone whose life is enriched through cultural and educational programs. When employees see that their company invests in and supports the community and its citizens, they feel good about working for the company. By fostering loyalty to the company in this way, businesses are positioned to attract and retain the best employees. This benefit is so great that many companies provide paid time off for employees to volunteer and also provide financial contributions to the nonprofits at which they volunteer.

Human resource executives, especially those responsible for leadership development, are often the best advocates for employee volunteerism. Shelley Seifert, senior vice president, human resources, at National City Bank in Cleveland, Ohio, reports that "employees will favor a workplace environment that encourages and supports community service" (interview, May 4, 2004). The findings of a survey of CEOs conducted for the World Economic Forum in January 2004 provide support for this point. According to the report, *Responding to the Leadership Challenge*, one of the factors they cite most commonly in making the case for their companies' citizenship activities is "attracting, motivating and retaining talented employees." The report indicates that "graduates increasingly value the ethical record and integrity of a company when choosing whom to work for. Corporate citizenship has also proven to be important in motivating and retaining key employees, which can be particularly important in times of economic uncertainty" (p. 14). Furthermore, according to BP Amoco, "We believe our employees' motivation is integral to the way in which the group performs. Empowered and committed people help to create a competitive advantage" *(BPAmocoAlive: Environmental and Social Update*, 2003, p. 3).

Yet another benefit of volunteerism is the sense of community it gives to a person who has moved from city to city. One consultant with a large national firm had lived in fifteen different cities before he moved to the Midwest ten years ago. Two years ago, on a Sunday morning, the consultant's house catastrophically burned to the ground, and the neighbors rallied around to help him and his young family for the entire day. The consultant's five-year-old son exclaimed, "This was the best day of my whole life!" At that moment, the consultant realized how much he wanted to contribute to his community. Not long after, he joined the board of a social service fundraising foundation where he provides his strategic skills in helping to shape the campaign to support important nonprofit services throughout the region.

According to management guru Rosabeth Moss Kanter, "The one goal for community service is employee relations: supporting employees who live in a community in their service to it, making them feel proud to work for the company because of what it contributes to local quality of life" (Moss Kanter, 1995, p. 194).

Building Visibility and Good Will

Employers realize that by supporting productive and meaningful community service, the company will establish good will in the communities where their employees and customers live and work. People who make a meaningful contribution of their time and talent on nonprofit boards are recognized at public events, in the media, and by fellow professionals from other businesses that also serve on boards. A corporate culture of service fosters good will in good times and can even serve as "crisis glue" when there are layoffs or bad press. Business volunteerism not only strengthens local relations but can also affect a company's national standing.

Those who study branding and market research affirm that companies can add value to their brand and reputation by making a valuable contribution to the community through lending their skills and expertise as well as cash. According to Carol Cone, Mark Feldman, and Alison DaSilva, "It's easy to say that companies should increase their giving, but what they really need to do is increase the types of support and better leverage their existing assets. Bringing skills and resources to a cause can inspire an entire community of employees, suppliers, customers, and public officials to make the cause their own. Each of these individuals in turn interacts with people further afield. Support for the cause then spreads, and the brand is more widely propagated" (2003, p. 5). Many companies are beginning to realize that comprehensive community-involvement strategies yield greater benefits than simply giving money. "Long-lasting community involvement programs are more likely to improve the image of the corporation than after-profit cash contributions. This is a reflection of the basic sentiment that people need help solving their problems, not just money" (Hess, Rogovsky, and Dunfee, 2002, p. 113).

Furthermore, visibility can be enhanced greatly when senior executives volunteer. According to Kenneth May, senior vice president of U.S. Operations, FedEx Corporation, both Frederick Smith, chairman and CEO of FedEx Corporation, and David Bronczek, CEO and president of FedEx Express, serve on boards and participate in volunteer activities (interview, June 7, 2004).

Promoting Economic Development

With few exceptions, employers such as banks, newspapers, professional-services firms, and manufacturers depend on a healthy local economy for their own businesses to succeed. Companies need an educated and healthy workforce; quality day care and education for the children of employees; pleasant and reliable senior homes and services; services for the homeless, mentally ill, and drug-addicted; and vibrant cultural centers and activities for people of all ages to enjoy. Furthermore, nonprofits that advance people from welfare to work increase the rate of employment through training and placement services; people who were previously jobless and dependent on welfare become taxpayers, homeowners, and retail customers.

For these reasons, businesses have a true incentive to be active in civic development, and awareness of this imperative is coming to the forefront at business conferences. "No company can do well if the community in which they operate is unhealthy," noted panelists at the 2002 Business Leadership Forum ("2002 Business Leadership Forum Monograph," 2002, p. 2).

Understanding How to Involve Businesses

Nonprofits need to realize that businesses' interests in becoming involved will vary depending on the nature of their work, culture, and leadership. For example, a professional-services firm may be interested in expanding public awareness of the caliber of their consultants; a manufacturing company may be interested in fostering employee loyalty in order to support recruitment, retention, and productivity; a bank may be focused on the vibrancy of the business community as well as on having an educated and well-prepared workforce; the local newspaper usually is most heavily invested in the overall economic welfare of the community because newspaper and advertising sales are local.

In addition different people and departments within each company may have different interests in community service. Public-relations officers understand the opportunity to develop good will. Executives in human resources and leadership development often realize that community service enhances personal and professional development, team building, and loyalty to the company. Marketing directors tend to recognize that consumers like to make purchases from companies that are perceived to be good corporate citizens. Community-relations officers, who often head the company foundation, are interested in leveraging corporate philanthropic dollars by involving their people as well as the company wallet. The CEO often has the bird's-eye view, understanding the range of benefits to the company as well as the value in helping to strengthen the community. Companies that are well organized have integrated community-involvement strategies that involve all the departments noted above, but in many corporations, one of these departments takes the lead. Therefore, nonprofit organizations that want to access business support need to decipher the political landscape of each company.

Small businesses tend to regard community service as a way to build teams, improve morale, and foster personal and professional development. Scott and Robert Durham, co-owners of a family printing business, HKM Direct Market Communications, Inc., in Cleveland, Ohio, enjoy their personal involvement on nonprofit boards, encourage employee volunteering as a team-building activity, and realize that other companies recognize and respect their company for their commitment. At the same time, the Durham brothers each has chosen boards where they feel a personal passion for the mission, and their enthusiasm drives their effectiveness. Both are recognized by the boards and chief executives for their leadership in fundraising, one at a crisis nursery shelter, and one at a major public health care institution (interview with chief executive of MetroHealth Foundation, November 17, 2004, and panel comments of chief executive of Providence House, September 10, 2004). Joel Marx, owner of Integrated Medical Services in Cleveland, Ohio, another family business, believes that his employees are enthusiastic about the company's interest in the community and relish opportunities to volunteer as a team (panel comments, Joel Marx, September 9, 2004).

Mid-sized businesses often present great opportunities for nonprofits seeking to access talent and support. Companies with fifty to a hundred employees are often untapped and quite enthusiastic about the chance to participate in meaningful community work. Their interests are similar to those of smaller and larger businesses; mid-size companies seek to enhance team-building and morale and provide an opportunity for employees who want to volunteer with their families. What makes the mid-size companies important in this equation is that they are so often missed in the rush to engage the larger, more visible, name-brand companies. Furthermore, executives from mid-size companies can be best attuned to the strategic challenges of nonprofits with fifty to a hundred employees.

Most companies have expectations of public recognition. Often, benefiting nonprofits can easily thank corporate donors and volunteers in their literature, on their websites, and in their press releases. Some companies ask a staff person from the nonprofit to attend a volunteer-recognition event, sponsored by the company at a company site, in order to thank employees for their volunteer time and contributions. A thoughtfully worded thank you letter that can be circulated to employees is often most touching and appreciated.

Understanding the Motivations of the Volunteers Themselves

In order to access and retain talented executives, nonprofits also need to consider the goals of individual volunteers and what they need to know in order to make the commitment. So many people are looking for ways to make a contribution that will advance a cause they can care about. They want to be useful, to make a difference. For example, Douglas Weill, managing director, real estate private fund group, at Credit Suisse First Boston LLC in New York City, notes that "I am especially interested in helping a smaller organization where I can help develop and grow the organization. I want to contribute my energy and experience where I can really be useful" (interview, November 12, 2004).

One business volunteer, Rick Mordesovich, managing director, Bank of America in San Francisco, who has served on boards in three cities while advancing in his profession, describes his nonprofit participation as his "volunteer career."

> I first served on a board in 1994. I was a young investment advisor looking to give back to the community. A board-matching service involved me on the board of a

center for the prevention of domestic violence. There, I
helped develop and launch the first of what has become
a very successful, annual fund-raising luncheon. This
experience was so rewarding that when I moved to
Chicago two years later, I joined the Northwestern
Memorial Hospital Board for planned giving. Today, in
San Francisco, I am involved with the Academy of
Friends and Friends of the Children. In my professional
life, I help families with complex issues around money
and philanthropy, so my volunteer experience has been
an important part of my learning and development. At
the same time, I have been able to play a role in helping each of the nonprofits I have served [interview, September 20, 2004].

A world-famous restaurateur once noted that "I don't sell meals.
I sell an experience." People are drawn to places and organizations
where the experience is positive. Nonprofits have the best opportunity of all to be the places where people have meaningful and
memorable experiences. Simply by making sure that volunteers
have a chance to be useful, nonprofits can draw extraordinary people of all ages and from all walks of life to participate in good causes.

Candidates also appreciate knowing what is expected of them
when they take on a management-assistance assignment or join a
board. Nonprofits can make themselves attractive to volunteers by
being clear about the "job description," respecting the volunteer's
time by starting and ending meetings as scheduled, and making
some logical adjustments, such as moving board meetings to times
that are "family-friendly" (5:30 to 7:00 P.M. so that members can go
home for dinner, instead of 8:00 P.M., which cuts into family time).

In order to maximize the value of the volunteers and to create
an environment that is welcoming, nonprofits can take the following measures:

- Assess the organization's scope and range of needs for volunteers, and be creative in considering potential volunteer opportunities—from done-in-a-day projects to management assistance to board service.

- Articulate the role of each category of volunteer— tutor, legal adviser, board treasurer—so that the job and the expectations are perfectly clear.

- Provide training for volunteers where needed, especially for tutors and those providing other direct client services.

- Make clear to the volunteers that the organization is counting on the services they have committed to provide.

- Provide a staff contact person at the nonprofit to serve as a resource to the volunteer. For a team project, an administrative assistant might be responsible for co-ordination. For management assistance, the contact would be the appropriate professional on staff at the nonprofit. For board involvement, the contact should be the chief executive.

- Decide how volunteers will be thanked and recognized. For example, a company team that builds a playground would probably enjoy a photo of the team next to the completed project and perhaps recognition in the non-profit newsletter or website. A board member might appreciate a small plaque or paperweight with the organization's logo and the volunteer's name. All volunteers love t-shirts!

Although it is important for nonprofit organizations to deter-mine how volunteers can be useful and to be creative in finding ways to involve them, nonprofits should not be expected to cater to volunteers at the expense of the organization. Sometimes businesses expect a nonprofit to invent a project to accommodate a large group of volunteers when the nonprofit site, programs, clients, and staff are not oriented to suit this demand. In such cases, nonprofit organizations need to be clear about what they can do and what they cannot do to create volunteer opportunities. Often, businesses themselves need guidance as to how they can be constructive and useful. Nonprofits can respond to corporate interests by suggesting a few alternative opportunities, such as a series of small projects.

Business volunteers often do more to assist nonprofits than they originally planned. For example, a group of employees from Continental Airlines volunteered one weekend to paint and decorate a playroom at a children's center. While they were there, one of the volunteers noticed that the washing machine was broken. The following Monday, the volunteer team raised enough money from co-workers to buy a new washer and dryer for the organization. Now the volunteers return twice each year to repair the roof, paint the rooms, and do a variety of hands-on projects. The attachment that has developed between the volunteers and the agency demonstrates that the volunteers felt their contributions were meaningful and derived a personal sense of satisfaction and reward.

Recognizing the Value of Volunteer Activities to Businesses

Nonprofit organizations are often painfully aware that they need financial support as well as volunteer time for board service and management assistance from businesses. But nonprofits should not underestimate the value they have to offer to businesses and businesspeople when they involve volunteers in meaningful service. Nonprofits can add value to businesses by engaging their employees in problem solving, governance, and done-in-a-day team-building activities. Service also adds a new dimension to the lives of the volunteers themselves. It is striking to see how many executives return to support a nonprofit that helped them when they were young. Organizations like the Boys & Girls Clubs of America and the YMCA are often the beneficiaries of the good will of successful adults who want to thank and recognize these organizations for having an impact on their lives. These executives talk about the personal rewards and satisfaction they derive from being useful and productive in helping others. Nonprofit organizations provide a powerful vehicle for human beings to be generous of spirit.

Often people who volunteer to provide their personal expertise to address a business problem at a nonprofit are astounded at how appreciative the organization is for assistance that is normally quite routine work for the volunteer. Many volunteers are touched by their ability to be so useful by performing an assignment that seems simple to them, especially when they assist with sophisticated matters in law, finance, human resources, marketing, and other related matters.

Engaging a Matchmaker

Another important part of this equation is the matchmaker, the person or organization that serves as the conduit between the business and nonprofit sectors. Many communities have nonprofit resource centers—themselves nonprofit organizations that are designed to provide management assistance and training services for nonprofits. Most communities also have at least one center whose role is volunteer matching. Nonprofit resource centers can conduct needs assessments of each nonprofit seeking assistance, interview each business volunteer who brings professional skills and expertise to the table, make the appropriate connections, and train new board members.

Nonprofits welcome introductions from matchmakers to volunteer consultants and board candidates who are screened and referred on the basis of the needs of the nonprofit. Nonprofits want board candidates and management-assistance volunteers who understand the nonprofit environment and its unique challenges. Furthermore, businesses eagerly welcome the expertise of an intermediary who understands the nonprofit sector and who can direct them and their employees to productive service opportunities. Having a highly effective matchmaker in a community leverages the interest of all parties in strengthening the community.

Recognizing the Importance of Measuring Impacts

Few deny that community service is a good thing. However, nonprofits should understand that corporate support for community involvement is strengthened if its value is measured and documented. Quite simply, companies are more likely to invest more seriously in initiatives that produce measurable results. A. Korngold and E. Voudouris explain the importance of quantifying the benefits of corporate community service as follows:

> Impact evaluation is essential to the effectiveness and viability of corporate community involvement. While many companies accept the premise that volunteerism is good for business, it is important to establish mechanisms to document and measure the benefits to the company, employees, and the community. After all, in other corporate endeavors, top management expects consistent reporting from all departments in order to determine where resources should be allocated, which programs are effective, and which initiatives should be continued. Furthermore, a carefully documented evaluation of the program's impact provides information that is needed in order to enhance opportunities to serve corporate and community interest. Finally, a report of the program's impact reinforces volunteers, inspires others to join in the effort, increases the program's visibility, strengthens support for the program both internally and

externally, and maximizes the public relations benefits
to the company [Korngold and Voudouris, 1996, p. 35].

Nonprofits are not in a position to measure the benefits to businesses, but it helps for nonprofits to understand the compulsion of
companies to do so. Measurement is important for a number of reasons. First, top management expects consistent reporting from all
departments in order to determine where resources will be allocated,
which programs are effective, and what programs to continue. Second, evaluating the community-involvement program's past and
present helps enhance the program in the future through continuous quality improvement. Third, reporting on the program's impact
increases visibility and enhances support in the company among
employees and senior management. Finally, reporting on the program's impact expands public-relations opportunities for the company. Impact measurement for businesses involves four steps:

- Determining and articulating the goals of the corporate
  community-involvement strategy

- Determining what to measure in order to assess the
  extent to which goals were achieved

- Developing a method to gather the data

- Deciding how the information will be used

Korngold and Voudouris designed an impact-evaluation model
for businesses. The model included five phases (1996, pp. 35–38).

1. Record keeping: A number of goals can be measured with
   simple record-keeping systems. Companies should track
   volunteer activities, number of volunteers involved, projects
   completed, nonprofits served, total volunteer hours, and the
   value of the time.

2. Process evaluation: Companies should assess the effectiveness of the structure, policies, and administration of the company's community-involvement program in order to ensure that employees have access to volunteer opportunities that meet their interests. It is useful to establish a volunteer advisory committee of employees; they can determine the features of the company's program that have been successful and ways to further improve the program.

3. Impact on employees: Companies should survey employees to see what they wish to accomplish through their volunteer efforts, and then circle back to employees to assess the extent to which the program has been effective in serving employee interests. For example, some employees prefer family-friendly volunteer projects for convenience and also to engage their children. Another employee goal might be to become better acquainted with fellow employees.

4. Impact on the company: In establishing their community-involvement programs, companies should clarify the benefits they expect. The company can also put in place systems to track a program's success. Human resource benefits can be evaluated through surveys and focus groups. Marketing benefits can be assessed through customer surveys. Companies can easily track the number of media features and mentions that result from their involvement in the community. All these results should be tracked and reviewed as part of the impact-evaluation process.

5. Impact on the community: Companies are especially interested in measuring their effectiveness in addressing key community issues. Some contributions can in fact be measured. One group of volunteers tutored children in an inner-city school with the majority of its pupils from families living under the poverty line; the volunteers noted improvements in the reading-proficiency test results of the children they

tutored compared with the children who did not have tutors, and the difference was dramatic. Other volunteer projects, such as building a playground, provide visible results, and by counting the number of children in the corresponding school or neighborhood who benefit a company can measure the impact. When volunteers provide management assistance, often their contributions can be measured in dollars saved or dollars raised. In other cases, it is difficult or impossible to measure outcomes. Companies should make the best attempt to look at the scope of volunteer contributions and estimate the aggregate value. This information will make employees feel proud and productive, while showing the company's good will to the community. Furthermore, companies that involve themselves and then measure and report serve as an inspiration to other businesses.

Impact evaluation might seem crass, but information that shows value, benefits, and outcomes is most likely to reinforce corporate interest in community involvement, bolster those who have supported volunteerism on good faith, and encourage many more companies to engage in similar activities. Businesses rely on information for decision making. Outcome data can often serve as a lever to move businesses to invest even further in nonprofits. Although nonprofits cannot assume this burden, it helps for nonprofits to recognize how and why businesses like to measure the outcomes of their participation in service.

The Bottom Line

Businesses seek to develop leadership, enhance team building, foster loyalty to the company, build visibility and good will, and improve the quality of life in their communities. They realize that through effective community service, they can develop their employees and corporate culture while also playing a strategic role in improving the communities where they do business. As Vartan

Gregorian, president and CEO of the Carnegie Corporation Foundation, states, "It's clear that we in the nonprofit sector are one of the central engines of our participatory democracy, making our country a world leader in addressing societal problems" (Gregorian, 2000).

By understanding the motivations of volunteers and businesses, nonprofits can involve thousands of volunteers in productive and meaningful service. The nonprofit sector can thereby build its capability and capacity to provide vital services. Matchmakers can make this dream a reality by serving as the conduit between the business and nonprofit sectors, facilitating good matches, and ensuring the win-win-win among businesses, nonprofits, and ultimately and most importantly, the community.

3

Making the Match

*The [nonprofit] sector enhances our creativity,
enlivens our communities, nurtures individual responsibility, stirs life at the grass roots, and reminds us
that we were born free. Its vitality is rooted in good
soil—civic pride, compassion, a philanthropic tradi-
tion, a strong problem-solving impulse, a sense of
individual responsibility and, despite what cynics may
say, an irrepressible commitment to the great shared
task of improving our life together.*
—John W. Gardner, Living, Leading,
and the American Dream, 2003

Nonprofits should consider "business volunteers" to include all professionals who bring business skills to the table, such as faculty and administrators of colleges and universities, medical and administrative staff of health care institutions, people from government agencies and nonprofit institutions, as well as businesses of all sizes. The value is in engaging people who have expertise in strategy, communications, law, finance, accounting, education, and human resources, teaching them how to apply their knowledge in the nonprofit environment (see Chapter Four), and deploying them to help nonprofits to address strategic and financial challenges and opportunities.

Based on their experiences with volunteers good and bad, non-profits realize that the benefit of involving business volunteers will be fully realized only if candidates and organizations are matched thoughtfully and carefully. It is unfortunate when a person who wants to volunteer can't find a place that needs her. It may be even worse if she winds up with an organization that does not meet her expectations. An opportunity to leverage good will has been squandered, and a volunteer has been turned off, possibly for a long time. It is even more problematic when a well-meaning volunteer causes more harm than good because he misinterprets expectations or is placed in a volunteer job that does not fit his interests and skills. Many nonprofits are familiar with situations of this kind, in which a potential win-win deteriorates into a lose-lose. The nonprofit has wasted time and energy and may even have a messy situation to deal with (because of ill will or bad advice); the volunteer is frustrated; the volunteer's employer might even look bad; and the community is the ultimate loser in that the value of someone who wanted to help has been lost. Good matches take time and attention, and only good matches result in good results for the volunteer, the employer, the nonprofit, and, most of all, the community.

Organizations that are poised to take on the vital role of match-maker are nonprofits that are traditionally referred to as resource centers, management-assistance organizations, leadership development programs, and volunteer centers. These organizations, based in cities throughout the nation, often have relationships with non-profit organizations in their local communities, and some of them have staff with expertise in nonprofit organizational matters. In many cases, these local organizations need to increase their prominence, resources, capacity, and capability so that they can serve as the matchmakers for businesspeople who have valuable talents to offer to nonprofits in the community.

As we have seen, nonprofits can use the talents of business-people in two ways. One is on a project basis as management consultants. The other is on a long-term basis as members of the board.

Each of these volunteer opportunities can present problems for the organization, the employer, and the volunteer if businesspeople are not matched accurately to the organizations they wish to help.

Management Assistance

Using businesspeople as management consultants is a good choice for a nonprofit that has a specific assignment and for a volunteer who can make only a limited commitment of time. Examples include a human resources executive who helps develop a policies-and-procedures manual; an organizational planner who facilitates strategic planning; an attorney who helps update the by-laws or acquire a property; a financial consultant who assists in developing investment policies; a management consultant who assists in restructuring the staff to adjust to an increase or decrease in funding; a communications specialist who helps make the case to funders; an accountant who helps revise the organization's financial procedures or reformat the financial statements presented to the board; an information-technology specialist who studies options and recommends the best database system to meet the nonprofit's needs; an attorney who guides an organization in exploring strategic alliances.

At a time when nonprofits can benefit from those who are experienced in business strategy, it is tempting simply to throw open the doors to any and all who seek to volunteer their time and talent. Why not welcome all who will help? Surely, some might say, their expertise will be useful to any nonprofit.

Nonprofits and those who fund them should, however, be wary of such simple solutions. In fact, those who understand the complexities of nonprofits and the uniqueness of the nonprofit environment find it frightening to think of well-meaning MBA students and businesspeople jumping in here and there to "straighten out" nonprofits. The random acceptance of volunteer assistance can be disastrous. Well-meaning volunteers can cause damage by inserting themselves into nonprofits without sufficient preparation and knowledge about the background of the organization and its culture. Resulting conflicts can lead to tensions between the board and the executive or among staff members. Such bad experiences abound, and nonprofit executives swap stories about them.

Nonprofits inclined to accept any volunteer should consider the time and care that go into the identification and selection of paid consultants in the for-profit sector. Business CEOs and managers are extremely thoughtful as they go through this process. The business client first defines and articulates the assignment for the consulting firms who will bid on the work. Then the client sends out a request for proposals, interviews prospective consultants, and checks their references and work samples. Only then does the CEO or manager select the candidate who has demonstrated suitability for the assignment. Suitability includes the consultant's having experience and expertise with the particular challenges and work environment, a clear grasp of the client's interests, an understanding of the complexity and nuances of the assignment, good chemistry with the client, and comfort in the client's work culture. Contrast that procedure with the random process nonprofits often use to select a volunteer from business or a team of volunteers.

Volunteer consultants and hired consultants in the for-profit sector have different roles and different expectations. In the for-profit sector, the consultant is remunerated with cash. In the volunteer setting, the business volunteer may expect to be "remunerated" with great deference and honor. If the volunteer is indeed helpful, then the respect for the volunteer is more than well deserved. If, however, the consultant lacks the insight, intellect, or diplomacy to be useful, then the consultant can be toxic to the organization, and the chief executive or board members can find themselves in an awkward situation.

Businesspeople may also unintentionally mistake the nonprofit environment and the for-profit environment. Nonprofits may have to undo the damage caused by volunteers' recommendations to follow certain business principles that are not suitable in the nonprofit environment. For instance, in a business, a program that loses money on a regular basis is often simply cut. In the nonprofit sector, though, the core services usually do not generate any revenues from the clients themselves; and, therefore, an organization needs to explore a variety of funding sources or perhaps a strategic alliance before resorting to closing a vital program. For example, providing food and shelter to homeless people or providing crisis shelter to abused or abandoned babies will never generate money from the "customers," and these services certainly will not make a profit. If these were profitable enterprises, they would be restaurants and hotels!

Furthermore, business volunteers may not understands that the nonprofit sector has a different work culture, with a variety of reward systems that do not correspond to those in the for-profit sector. For example, in for-profits, good performance can be measured by sales and rewarded with financial incentives; in nonprofits, it can be considered unethical to give an executive a bonus based on private donations or community grants. Additionally, the auxiliary "sales force" for a nonprofit is the board members in that their role is to contribute and raise funds; their incentive is purely psychic, or pride-based, and not financial. Board members are likely to strive hardest when they are inspired by good leaders and pressured by peers, instead of being paid bonuses (*Code of Ethical Principles and Standards of Professional Practice*, 2002).

Businesspeople who volunteer at nonprofits often make several false assumptions. First, they often anticipate that the nonprofit environment is simpler than the for-profit sector when in fact it is far more complex. For example, management consultants who are accustomed to dealing with Fortune 500 companies and company budgets of hundreds of millions or billions of dollars sometimes think that dealing with a social services organization with an operating budget of $10 million will be child's play. They are often humbled when they see that the nonprofit's financial statements show several different third-party payers (the county, the state, and various managed-care organizations) and then learn that each of these funding sources has unique and highly complex expectations of the nonprofit with regard to reporting systems and pay-out timetables. Even worse, the nonprofit may be expected to provide certain services, such as day care, only to find that the reimbursement rate has been cut by the funding source after the service has been provided. For many nonprofits, a series of after-the-fact cuts like that can put the organization is serious jeopardy. Business volunteers' assumptions about the simplicity of the nonprofit sector are often challenged once they get involved. In fact, in a survey of business executives and professionals trained and placed on nonprofit boards in 2002–2003, 49 percent reported that the issues of the organizations they served were "more complex than they had expected." The majority of these people had had several years of business experience, and many had graduate degrees in business or law (*BVU Survey of Board Candidates Elected Through BVU, 2002-2003*).

Second, businesspeople often assume that their business skills will readily transfer to the nonprofit environment. Although volunteers' experiences can be quite useful, they need first to educate themselves about a nonprofit's unique circumstances. According to Eugene Lang, founder and chairman emeritus of the "I Have a Dream" Foundation, who has successfully led many international business enterprises, "When a business person enters a new market, he knows what he needs to learn. In the nonprofit environment, it may take a while for the volunteer to figure out what he needs to learn" (interview, 2004). For example, a marketing consultant who is accustomed to promoting consumer goods, such as home furnishings, has certain understandings of supply and demand. The volunteer may find that expanding the community's support for a baroque orchestra, engaging the next generation of young people in appreciating the musical arts, and convincing donors and foundations that a quality music ensemble is good for economic development requires a different understanding of supply and demand.

A common dilemma for arts organizations is how to present the "same old" Christmas performance that is sure to sell seats, while also fulfilling their educational mission to expand the community's horizons by introducing newer, more thought-provoking material. If all arts organizations felt compelled to repeat the same narrow but highly popular repertory, then the public would only hear Beethoven's Fifth Symphony, see the Nutcracker ballet, watch A *Christmas Carol*, and see Monet paintings (in the few cities that can afford to have Monets). How would we ever become exposed to a variety of artists and perspectives? How would we see plays about the African American experience, attend experimental theater performances, hear the works of contemporary composers, see paintings by new artists, and view installations of extraordinary sculptures? In fact, without nonprofit support, many less mainstream artists would lose patrons and be unable to enrich the arts as well. "Selling" cultural learning is not the same as selling houses or toothpaste.

In one case, a business volunteer offered to assist the regional ballet company. He was a seven-year veteran in one of the nation's top management-consulting firms with advanced degrees in engineering and business. He was struck by the fact that in order to develop a marketing plan for the ballet to build audience, he could not use the usual approaches to measure the community's need for and interest in this product. He was faced with the challenge of promoting a product for which there was no clearly identified market or "need."

Third, businesspeople often assume that nonprofits and their staffs do not know what they are doing. Underlying this notion is the belief, discussed above, that because nonprofits are often small enterprises, they must be simple to operate. In fact, many people who run nonprofits have extraordinary experience in their fields. Lang's advice is to "respect the professionals who work on the front lines" (interview, Eugene Lang, March 3, 2004). In fact, once businesspeople get involved as volunteers, they are usually surprised to learn that nonprofit staffs know a great deal about the sector and its problems, and nonprofit executives are usually stunningly creative in sustaining services in the face of powerful threats.

Many nonprofits fully realize that they can benefit tremendously from the involvement of business volunteers. At the same time, nonprofits expect volunteers to approach a nonprofit assignment with some degree of humility and an openness to learn about the nonprofit sector and its unique challenges and circumstances. Business volunteers who enter into the nonprofit realm with an open mind usually find that they are the ones who have the learning experience.

Board Membership

Although poorly matched volunteer consultants can be troubling and harmful, badly matched board members can be even more disastrous for the organization and ultimately the community. Here again, employers sometimes make the faulty and dangerous assumption that any random businessperson will bring value to a board. Underlying this assumption is a patronizing and condescending attitude toward nonprofits and an overinflated view of businesspeople (one need only read the *Wall Street Journal* for tales of low-performing companies and individuals).

Nonprofits should be cautious about opening their boardrooms; on-line matching as a source of board candidates is particularly treacherous. People who join boards via on-line matching often do not have sufficient understanding of the circumstances of the organization and its culture; even worse, the nonprofits do not have sufficient information about the candidates, their personalities, their true qualifications and styles of working. In this era of Sarbanes-Oxley (federal legislation that set new standards of performance and accountability for public companies), even for-profits that have been devoting time and resources to rigorous board-member searches are recognizing that their approaches need to be improved.

In response to increased demands for public accountability, for-profits are becoming more purposeful in identifying board candidates. At the same time some nonprofits are being offered candidates through an on-line process! Imagine for-profit boards engaging people through the internet, rather than through an executive search.

Nonprofit boards are learning that the traditional approach of gathering a random group of vaguely interested people—usually friends and acquaintances—is simply not effective. Instead, nonprofits should build their boards purposefully with people who have a passion for the cause and who bring the specific experience and expertise that is needed to make key organizational decisions regarding mission, strategic direction, community relationships, communications, and revenue models. Nonprofits should also encourage board candidates themselves to be selective in choosing where they will serve based on their personal interests, as well as an understanding of their role. According to the editor of a business journal, "If you don't believe in an organization's mission or feel like you can connect with its audience, you won't get the most out of the experience. And the organization probably won't get the most out of you" (Klein, 2002, p. 40). Board candidates should consider a variety of options in order to choose where they can best contribute.

The Value of the Matchmaker

As mentioned in Chapters One and Two, matchmakers can play a vital role in helping nonprofits and volunteers find the right fit; the right fit can boost the nonprofit's success while satisfying the need of the volunteer to make a meaningful contribution.

Many businesspeople who would like to help simply do not know how to access suitable opportunities. A software business-person in Silicon Valley attended a national conference of nonprofit organizations to find organizations that might accept his company's pro-bono website services. He explained that when he cold-called nonprofits to offer assistance, they did not trust him. After a few attempts, he was reasonable and patient enough to realize that nonprofits have reason to be skeptical and that he needed an "honest broker." One knowledgeable conference participant suggested that he get in touch with CompassPoint, a nonprofit resource center in San Francisco, to find assistance in making the right connections. Without matchmakers, nonprofits lose good will. Most business volunteers do not have the time and resources of the person described above. For nonprofits, these are missed opportunities.

Nonprofits often call on community-relations specialists who are based at corporations to make board and volunteer matches for their companies. (Only the largest national and international corporations have dedicated staff in the area of community relations.) Although many of these corporate staff members are responsible for board matching (in addition to overseeing volunteerism and often corporate donations as well), and many have good knowledge of the nonprofit sector, they are among the first to say that they do not have the resources to conduct a proper needs assessment of each nonprofit that seeks executives for its board. Furthermore, it is almost impossible for them to be aware of all of the local community's needs. They thus have difficulty identifying the right candidate for a board. Additionally, community-relations staff often express the concern that the nonprofits' key interest is corporate funding and that that is the impetus for their request for board members.

Nonprofit organizations often call on nonprofit resource centers and volunteer centers for their recommendations for board members and volunteer consultants. Hundreds of cities in the United States have nonprofit resource centers, volunteer centers, corporate volunteerism councils, and other organizations whose missions involve volunteerism and nonprofit consulting. Unfortunately, many of these organizations are far too limited for them to play a significant role in making good matches. Nonprofits and their advocates should encourage foundations and philanthropies to build up these organizations for several reasons.

First, a fully-developed regional matchmaking service can establish a large pool of board and volunteer opportunities, on the one hand, and a large pool of candidates on the other hand; the result will be more options and, thus, better matches. A nonprofit seeking a board candidate or volunteer for management assistance will have the pick of candidates from a multitude of employers and sources in the community. The candidate seeking to volunteer for boards or management assistance will have hundreds of nonprofits from which to choose. With a sophisticated matching process, the right organization and the right individual are likely to be brought together. The outcome, then, is more fulfilling for everyone involved: the nonprofit gets optimal volunteer assistance; the volunteer can find the most rewarding place to make an impact; and everyone benefits from the matchmaker's training and consulting services (as discussed below).

Nonprofit organizations have an enormous range and scope. This book focuses on charitable organizations that have tax-exempt status in order to serve community interests. Key U.S. cities have thousands of such organizations, many of which are actively seeking board candidates and volunteer consultants. These organizations have annual operating budgets of seventy thousand to hundreds of millions of dollars. They include start-ups and well-established organizations, as well as many that are or will soon be in the throes of mergers. Nearly all the organizations are in some state of financial flux given the conditions noted in Chapter One.

So, nonprofit organizations vary widely in mission, revenue model, composition and role of their boards, role of the chief executive, and size of their budgets. Given such a wide variety of options for boards and for candidates, extraordinary matches can occur through thoughtful matching processes. An example is a nonprofit fair-housing agency that promotes equal housing opportunities and positive race relations. The center's services include systemic and complaint-based discrimination testing, mapping and research, enforcement of the Fair Housing Act through litigation, and education and outreach. With some hesitation and delay, the executive director sought a matchmaker's assistance in identifying board candidates; his reluctance was based on his doubts that any "corporate types" would be interested in a fair-housing initiative. Within days of conducting the needs assessment of the housing center, the matchmaker interviewed a member of the environmental-practice group of a law firm. She was a former college professor who had taught in the areas of city planning and urban design. She held a Ph.D. in history and city and regional planning and a J.D. Because of her background and professional interest in this field, she jumped at the opportunity to be introduced as a board candidate for the housing center. This kind of match is possible with a large pool of board candidates and a variety of nonprofits.

Second, an effective regional matchmaking service can help make boards more inclusive than they often are. Many nonprofit boards are limited in their candidate outreach because their own networks are too homogeneous. Local nonprofit resource centers that establish matchmaking services are positioned to create relationships with minority professional organizations and women's professional groups, which are vital sources of a diverse pool of board candidates. Regional matchmakers can expand the reach for all nonprofits by cultivating a large group of highly qualified and diverse candidates. For example, if a board that comprises older, founding families wants to engage younger and more diverse candidates in order to reach new and broader audiences, a regional matchmaker with access to hundreds of business candidates from a multitude of diverse professional societies and backgrounds is likely to be able to identify the right individuals.

Third, regional matchmaking services have expertise regarding nonprofits. They are often in the best position to develop a vast and sophisticated reservoir of expertise. The knowledge and experience of staff members at a nonprofit resource center can be useful in making suitable matches and preparing and coaching volunteer consultants and board members.

Fourth, a regional nonprofit resource center has the funding and expertise required to conduct needs assessments and to provide training. This not only is a high-quality approach but is also cost-effective. By meeting with the board and staff of each nonprofit client, matchmakers can determine exactly how volunteers might be useful. And matchmakers can also develop excellent training curricula and consulting services based on the major issues facing nonprofits.

A dedicated matchmaking center can serve nonprofits by creating a staff of experts to assist all parties in achieving the best outcome. As Figure 3.1 illustrates, matchmakers can serve as the fulcrum to leverage business talent to strengthen the nonprofit sector. Matchmakers can do so by drawing on skilled volunteers from employers throughout the community, developing the volunteers with training and coaching services, and providing management and board training and consulting services to nonprofits.

Making the Match

Given the challenges and complexities of the nonprofit sector, matchmakers must be highly qualified professionals, with graduate degrees, nonprofit board experience, and nonprofit management experience. Qualified matchmakers add value by identifying the

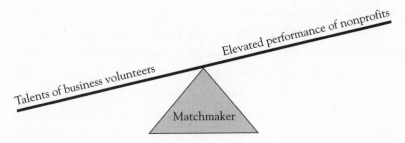

Figure 3.1. The Matchmaker as Fulcrum.

organization's key strategic issues, understanding the organization's board dynamic and culture, assessing the organization's needs for assistance, interviewing each board and volunteer candidate, and channeling useful help to the nonprofit. Matchmakers need to take the following key steps to achieve a good match between a volunteer candidate and a nonprofit organization.

1. Conduct a Needs Assessment of the Nonprofit

Nonprofits often need help in zeroing in on their key strategic issues and clarifying their needs for volunteer assistance. Often, when nonprofits call for help, they ask for fundraisers. By conducting a proper needs assessment, however, the matchmaker can determine specifically where the organization is hurting or vulnerable and identify people with the skills that will be most useful.

Good matches can be made only if matchmakers conduct face-to-face needs assessments of each nonprofit organization seeking assistance. Furthermore, the meeting should be conducted at the nonprofit site in order for the matchmaker to get a sense of the organization's environment and culture. In a 90–120-minute meeting with the board chair and chief executive of the nonprofit, a skilled matchmaker can gather the information necessary to hone in on the challenges and opportunities facing the organization. An experienced matchmaker will also be able to interpret the nuances of the dynamic between the board chair and the chief executive. The subtleties of the interpersonal relationships that can be seen in a face-to-face meeting cannot be grasped in an on-line communication or even by telephone.

Usually, the best way to identify the issues that matter most is to learn about the revenue model and understand the key sources of funding: which are strong, which are in jeopardy, and why. The matchmaker also needs to learn how the organization evaluates and communicates its value to key constituents. Finally, the matchmaker should gather basic information about the board meeting schedule, committees, expectations of board members, how board members meet those expectations, and what happens if they do not.

To learn about the organization, the matchmaker should spend a couple of hours reviewing basic organizational information and materials: the budget, board and executive committee minutes, strategic and financial plans (if they exist), promotional literature, and other related information. In addition, the matchmaker should meet with the board leadership (board chair or chair of the governance/nominating committee or both) and the nonprofit's chief executive for a couple of hours. In some cases, it is best to meet with the chief executive and board chair separately and in other cases to meet them together. This judgment is based on the initial call and conversation. For example, if the call is from a chief executive and one of the concerns is the attitude or commitment of the board chair, then separate meetings might yield more candid information than a joint meeting. In the same way, if the call is from a board chair who is not sure about the chief executive's effectiveness, separate meetings would likely be more valuable. An advantage to meeting the chair and chief executive together is to observe the interaction between them and to gauge their reactions to each other's comments about the organization. In any case, the perspectives of the board and the chief executive are necessary in order to gain a balanced perspective of the issues.

The meeting with the organization's leadership is especially useful in identifying the key strategic and financial challenges and opportunities; this meeting should also be used to review the board list (with each person's title and company/organization affiliation) in order to identify gaps in the skills and relationships that are needed for success. It is important to leave the meeting with a clear understanding of the organization's needs for talents and relationships.

The matchmaker needs to realize that the issue presented by the board chair or chief executive may merely be a symptom of systemic problems, rather than the core issue. By conducting the needs

assessment, the matchmaker can determine the key issues and identify the skill sets that will be most useful to the organization. For
example, a nonprofit that derives most of its funding through a fee-
for-service or third-party-payer reimbursement system may not be
accurately determining the costs of providing services, and thus revenues may not be keeping up with costs. This organization might
need a better tracking or information system to assess costs or, perhaps, a new pricing strategy. Or the organization might need to re-
organize its overall structure for increased efficiency in the delivery
of services. Yet another possibility is the need for a select group of
board members to join the chief executive in meeting with the primary funder—perhaps the county commissioners or the board of
education—to seek a remedy. Additional board fundraising may
be the solution or, more drastically, cutting a service, the last re-
sort. Sometimes the organization can no longer be viable as a free-
standing organization. In this case, the best help might be provided
by an attorney, a business consultant, and a financial analyst, who
are each expert in mergers.

By exploring the key issues, the professional conducting the
needs assessment can determine the kinds of experience required in
a volunteer management consultant or board member. Businesspeople who can be of service might include a financial analyst/
planner, a senior human resources executive, an organizational-
development specialist, a government-relations expert, or some
combination of these experiences. An organization needing to
expand its facilities might need board members or volunteer consultants in law, construction, real estate, finance, investments, and
the request-for-proposal process. An organization that is under-
resourced might need help in developing a communications strategy in order to convey the compelling value of the organization. In
this case, the key issue might also involve the need for outcome
measurement and reporting.

The needs assessment helps the matchmaker not only to determine the qualifications and experience needed in the volunteer but

also to communicate to potential volunteers the nature of the "assignment." By being clear about the work that the volunteer is needed for, the matchmaker can ensure the highest caliber match.

2. Interview Each Candidate

The matchmaker needs certain information about each candidate. An application form, on-line or on paper, can provide the matchmaker with sufficient information to create an initial list of organizations for discussion with the candidate. The application form provides the matchmaker with basic information about the volunteer's background and experience. Additionally, the application should provide information about the candidate's interest in various community issues as well as preference for the size, scope, and culture of the organization. Some candidates will have broader or less clearly defined interests, while others will be specific. Most will begin without any idea of the range and scope of volunteer opportunities, so this process becomes an educational and counseling experience with regard to the candidate's "volunteer career."

The matchmaker, though, should never make assumptions about a candidate's interests based on the profile. High-level corporate executives sometimes choose the boards of small, troubled organizations where they can make a difference rather than be another name on the board roster. Frequently, in fact, candidates say, "Refer me to a board where I can be most useful." One nationally known public-relations expert asked for a match to an organization that would present the greatest challenge. For people like these, the desire to make a meaningful contribution is often the predominant motivating factor.

The meeting between the matchmaker and candidate is essentially a counseling session to help the candidate consider various opportunities in light of interests and areas of expertise. Like a high-quality job interview or an executive search, this candidate assessment must be done face to face. The matchmaker should present several options to the candidate and listen carefully as the candidate thinks out loud about the options. The matchmaker should discuss each organization, its purpose, programs, services, budget size, challenges, opportunities, and culture. By listening, the matchmaker can gain an increased understanding of the candidate's interests and goals. Often, in the course of the meeting, the candidate will mention a variety of interests that did not come across in the written application. The matchmaker can then suggest organizations that he or she did not originally present to the candidate. It is an organic process. Furthermore, the matchmaker will get a sense of the candidate's style and personality, which can be important in matching a person to the culture of an organization.

The face-to-face interview can foster creative matches that might never have occurred otherwise. Candidates are often receptive to possibilities they never imagined. Occasionally, a candidate says, "Oh, my, that nonprofit is a mile from my house, and I pass it every day on my way to work. I never knew what they do." Sometimes a candidate may choose a particular board for personal involvement but eventually make financial contributions to other organizations discussed in the interview with the matchmaker.

In one case, the comptroller of a mid-size advertising firm who had several years of experience in finance and budgeting as well as an MBA identified several interest areas on her application, not including the performing arts. In the interview, she happened to mention that she had been a ballerina as a child. The matchmaker then suggested a board opportunity with a ballet company seeking someone with financial skills. The candidate, who was in her mid-thirties, had not considered serving on the ballet board because she assumed this board would be of too high a stature for her age and lack of board experience. Yet it turned out to be the perfect match; the candidate brought the exact skills that the organization had specified. She not only was elected to the board but was also asked to serve as the board treasurer within four months of joining. Another candidate, who was matched to an adoption agency that served interracial families, was inspired by his own experience as an

African American child raised by Caucasian parents. Yet another candidate was an amateur pianist who was matched to the board of a music conservatory for children.

The match needs to be made based on the organization's culture as well as its mission and purpose. Because of the matchmaker's visit to the nonprofit and meeting with the board and staff leadership, the matchmaker will be prepared to discuss the organizational environment with the candidate in order to facilitate a suitable match. The matchmaker can help the candidate get a feeling for the nonprofit by describing the organization's setting, services, and clients. One organization might serve troubled young people in a center located in a community facing poverty and urban tensions, while another organization that helps cancer patients and their families might be located in a serene suburban setting where it offers support groups and yoga classes.

Aside from setting, the board cultures and organizational issues of nonprofits differ. For example, a novice board candidate might not be the best fit for an organization that is in turmoil; a novice might be better suited to a more stable organizational environment that has more specific needs for expertise. A seasoned board member or a mergers-and-acquisitions attorney or consultant might be perfect for a board that is involved in or contemplating a complex and highly politicized strategic alliance. A board candidate who is eager to jump in and play a significant role might be less suited to a large, established organization than is someone who wants to learn about a more mature organization as well as seek out seasoned mentors.

3. Respect the Nonprofit's Right to Choose Its Volunteers

The terms *matching* and *placing* are easy to use, but not precise. The matchmaker's job should be to *identify* and *refer* candidates to nonprofits based on the interests and qualifications of each volunteer and the specific needs of each nonprofit. A nonprofit has complete discretion in choosing its board members or volunteer consultants. If there is any pressure at all on the nonprofit to elect candidates referred by the matchmaker, the nonprofit will not use the referral service. Furthermore, the matchmaker's integrity will be called into question if there is any perception that the referral is made for motives other than to introduce qualified candidates to nonprofits seeking assistance.

Given that a matchmaker cannot choose volunteers for a nonprofit, whom does the matchmaker serve—the candidate, the sponsoring business/employer, or the nonprofit? All three are clients of the matchmaker, and the interests of all parties must be respected equally. In practice, the matchmaking organization does its best to find a good volunteer opportunity for each candidate who is recommended by an employer and who follows through on the process by completing the application form and participating in the interview and the board training. At the same time, in the interest of all parties, the matchmaking organization should refer candidates to boards only when the matchmaker believes there will be a mutual interest. If the matchmaker refers candidates who are not properly qualified and interested to a board, then nonprofits will no longer use the service. If matchmakers refer candidates to organizations in which the candidates do not have an interest, then businesses will no longer use the service. If candidates are not prepared through good board training, then businesses, candidates, and nonprofits will not use the service. The matchmaker must practice with complete integrity and make referrals that are suitable for all parties.

For board referrals, the matchmaker should introduce the candidate to the nonprofit by sending information about the candidate to the board leaders (the chair or the nominating/governance committee chair or both) and to the nonprofit's chief executive for their review. If the organization is interested, then the board and staff leadership should meet with the candidate, recommend the candidate to the board through the organization's normal nominations process, and elect accordingly if they choose to do so. If the organization is not interested in the candidate, the matchmaker can pursue an alternative match for the candidate and the nonprofit. The value of having a central matchmaking service in each major U.S. community is the volume and range of board opportunities as well as the volume and variety of board candidates; with care and attention, there will be a good board match for every candidate.

In the case of a volunteer management consultant, the matchmaker will probably introduce the candidate only to the chief executive of the organization, rather than to board leaders, because the consultant will most likely work for the chief executive or one of the senior team members. It is often helpful for the matchmaker to attend this engagement meeting in order to ensure that there is a clear and common understanding of the volunteer assignment. Furthermore, the matchmaker should follow up with the nonprofit and the volunteer to ensure that the assignment is moving forward as planned. In some cases, the volunteer and the nonprofit may eventually decide on a longer-term relationship for volunteer consulting or board involvement.

For example, an organization received funding to increase its annual operating budget from $300,000 to $1 million. With the additional new funding, the organization increased its staff from three to ten people. Consequently, the organization sought a volunteer consultant to help establish a new management structure with job descriptions for each employee and personnel-performance systems. The matchmaker had previously interviewed a human resources consultant from a consulting firm that specialized in small and mid-size businesses. The consultant was experienced in this exact assignment with for-profits and had expressed interest in being useful to a nonprofit seeking this kind of expertise. The matchmaker began by calling the volunteer to make sure he would have an interest in helping this particular organization. Then the matchmaker sent the volunteer's resume to the chief executive of the nonprofit for her review. The nonprofit executive agreed that the volunteer appeared well qualified and agreed to meet with him and the matchmaker. In the course of the ninety-minute "engagement meeting," the matchmaker ascertained whether the volunteer could transfer his skills into the nonprofit environment. The nonprofit executive described the challenge and what she wanted from the volunteer. He responded with his understanding of the assignment and out-lined how he would help. It was evident from the discussion that the volunteer was aware of the issues and was presenting a good process for the organization to follow. The consultant was engaged. The matchmaker's role in the meeting was to make sure the volun-teer met the needs of the nonprofit executive. (If he did not, the matchmaker would seek another candidate, perhaps someone with a better understanding of the qualifications.)

If the matchmaker has done a good job of assessing the non-profit's needs and referring a candidate who has valuable qualifica-tions, the board election or volunteer engagement occurs in almost all cases. Good experiences and outcomes lead to trust and credi-bility for the matchmaker. This positive regard advances the match-maker's reputation and leads to increased use of the service and support for the matchmaking organization.

4. Train Board Candidates

The matchmaker needs to prepare board candidates for board ser-vice with an in-person, interactive training seminar. Although sev-eral books address the role of a nonprofit board, it is not sufficient to hand a new board member a book about boards and expect the kind of insight and participation that the board will need from its newest member. On-line training and discussion have their limita-tions as well. Written materials tend to describe how boards should function. In the real world, however, people are joining boards that are not functioning at the optimal level, and a board member who wants to make a difference needs to figure out how to navigate in the board environment. Cynthia Gibson, program officer at the Carnegie Corporation of New York, is a strong advocate for train-ing new board members. She comments that "the real value-added of a nonprofit matchmaking service is in board-candidate training.

With proper preparation for board service, business people can contribute useful perspectives and expertise" (interview, April 14, 2004).

Based on my experience in training over four thousand nonprofit board members at governance seminars, the most engaging and useful discussions take place when audiences comprise experienced board members as well as novices. Those who are already serving on boards, even for many years, are seeking enlightenment regarding best practices in nonprofit governance. This curiosity is driven by new challenges facing nonprofits and a greater interest on the part of boards to improve their effectiveness. By including experienced board members, the matchmaker not only increases learning for the novices but also provides a service to all board members in the community. The quality of the discussion is richer when half the audience has already faced difficult situations and can raise these dilemmas in the course of the seminar. In seminars that comprise only newly placed board members, the discussion is weaker because the audience does not have enough experience to know what to ask.

A well-designed board seminar will help board candidates begin to grasp the range and variety of experiences they might face on nonprofit boards, the complexities of the nonprofit sector, board dynamics, and ways to conduct oneself in order to be an effective board member. By interacting in a three-hour session with experienced board members and chief executives of nonprofits, new board members can begin to learn from real-world situations and begin to think about problem solving, group dynamics, and boardroom culture. This is the best preparation for candidates who are about to attend their first board meeting, which may otherwise be a mystery. Consequently, the new board member can add value to the organization sooner rather than later, thoughtfully rather than clumsily. Effective board preparation can minimize the trial-and-error process for the board candidate and the nonprofit.

Additionally, a good board seminar will help board members— new and experienced—understand that the unexpected is to be expected, that they are not alone, and that organizational advancement can be achieved. A good board seminar will help board members realize their potential to become change agents as long as they approach the group with care and sensitivity and an eye on the greater good.

A good board seminar includes a panel of experienced board members who have served in board leadership positions as well as chief executives of nonprofits. Experienced funders are also good panelists. The program should be designed for an audience of sixty-five to eighty-five people in order to ensure a certain level of energy and engagement among a diverse group of individuals. A smaller group will reveal fewer viewpoints; a larger group will present difficulties for participation.

The format should balance brief plenary presentations, interactive discussions, and small-group discussions, thereby providing a variety of media for learning. The agenda should begin with a concise overview of the challenges and opportunities facing the nonprofit sector, a summary of board-member roles and responsibilities, and a presentation by an attorney about the duties of care, loyalty, and obedience. This legal presentation is essential. On the one hand, clarity about legal responsibilities dissuades anyone who might think that attendance at board meetings is discretionary; on the other hand, clarity alleviates the anxieties of those who seriously want to know what they are getting into. There should be no more than forty-five minutes of presentation before the group is directly engaged in discussion; longer than that, and audience attention dissipates.

The centerpiece of the seminar should be an interactive discussion between the audience and the panel of skilled nonprofit leaders. The choice of panelists and the level of discussion should appeal to a sophisticated group of experienced board members, businesspeople who are joining boards for the first time, and chief executives of nonprofits. The discussion should be facilitated by a dynamic leader who has served on boards, led nonprofit organizations, consulted to boards, and served as a presenter and facilitator. The facilitator needs to make sure that certain matters—strategic alliances, financial oversight, fundraising, board composition, and roles of board committees—are addressed in the course of the discussion. At the same time, the facilitator should encourage and support a conversation that moves at a fast pace. In particular, the facilitator needs to make sure that the panel addresses issues from the perspective of large and small organizations, from the perspective of the chief executive as well as of the board, and from the vantage point of cultural organizations as well as organizations that focus on health and human services. Panelists should be encouraged to offer conflicting points of view based on their experiences. For example, it is helpful for the audience to hear the pros and cons of term limits or panelists' anecdotes about their experiences in forging strategic alliances or reducing or increasing the size of an organization. The more diverse the panel experiences and perspectives, the richer the learning and the more dynamic the seminar experience. People are pleased to be invited to serve on "role-of-the-board" panels because of the opportunity to help prepare others for board service.

The seminar should also allow members of the audience to split into smaller groups with panelists for case-study analysis. These groups provide an additional opportunity for participants to engage in problem solving with the guidance of a skilled facilitator.

The matchmaker should also provide an array of a la carte seminars that focus on specific issues such as financial oversight, strategic alliances, and effective leadership. By listening to the concerns and interests of nonprofit board members, matchmakers can design forums to address the most pressing issues. All the seminars should be taught and facilitated by groomed experts who are also excellent teachers.

With proper preparation and follow-up coaching, board members who attend these seminars can become change agents and draw fellow board members into adopting best practices.

5. Provide Complementary Board Consulting Services

Engaging qualified people on boards is a major step in strengthening boards. Training board candidates is another important step. Yet another vital piece is providing high-quality board training and consulting services. Matchmaking programs should be integrated with training and consulting services that help board members understand their roles, define governance agendas, form effective committee structures, clarify board-member expectations, and provide good orientation and education programs. One substantial organization in each major community can provide one-stop access for nonprofits seeking assistance; concentrate nonprofit expertise for matchmaking, consulting, and training; and consolidate and leverage funding for high-quality, high-stature services to strengthen nonprofits.

Furthermore, candidates who are trained and placed on boards often recognize the nonprofit's needs for board-development services; these board members will turn to the matchmaking organization for help. According to a survey of candidates placed on boards, 40 percent indicated that the boards they serve needed consulting; 53 percent indicated that their boards needed training; 77 percent indicated that their boards needed additional candidates from a qualified matchmaker; and 26 percent indicated that their organizations needed management assistance. In fact, every one of the 267 organizations that elected board candidates or engaged volunteer consultants through a sophisticated matchmaker also opted to use a nonprofit resource center for board or management training or consulting (*BVU Survey of Board Candidates Elected Through BVU*, 2002–2003).

Local Nonprofit Resource Centers as Matchmakers

As noted earlier, hundreds of communities have nonprofit organizations that are designated as resource centers. They provide management training and consulting for nonprofits. Many other volunteer-matching services are also nonprofits themselves. Unfortunately, these organizations are under-resourced. Resource centers that become matchmakers to leverage businesses to help nonprofits need to be elevated to gain the respect of businesspeople who are interested in serving on nonprofit boards, nonprofit executives, community foundations, and private and corporate funders. The matchmaker's training and consulting services need to be provided by expert facilitators who have advanced degrees in business management, nonprofit management, and experience in leading and consulting to nonprofit organizations. Serious funding is required to support the work of these centers. Annual operating budgets of $2–$3 million annually would be required to fund matchmakers in each major U.S. city; they could then hire and retain qualified staff members to provide matching services as well as board consulting and training.

The elevation of resource centers in quality and scope of services, stature, and role in the community can occur only with increased investment by foundations and corporations as well as leadership from people of influence. In order to achieve the necessary prominence in the community, the boards of directors of nonprofit resource centers need to be properly positioned to generate substantial resources. The boards need to comprise people in high positions who see the challenges and opportunities facing nonprofits and have the bold vision to build superior services to strengthen the nonprofit sector.

It is alarming that the nation's most important programs and services are provided by small nonprofit organizations (most with annual budgets well under $1 million) without access to the professional training, consulting, and board-matching services that are needed in order to address the serious and complex challenges described in Chapter One. Contrast their situation with that of the for-profit consulting industry, with firms such as McKinsey, Bain, Boston Consulting Group, and others generating hundreds of millions of dollars in fees. Consider the extraordinary qualifications of the consultants who come from the nation's top universities and graduate programs and who receive significant salaries. Consider the training and mentoring that the for-profit firms invest in their consultants. The contrast with the limited resources for the development of nonprofit organizations is astounding. In fact, it is incredible that nonprofits function as well as they do without the robust and excellent professional services that are provided to for-profits.

It is thus important to strengthen matchmaker organizations and to do so at the local level. Even though many of the challenges facing nonprofits have a degree of universality, nonprofits usually need to build boards and address issues within the regional context. This local context is important because most of the client organizations' funders are likely to be community foundations, local private philanthropists, and county and state governments, and local boards will be attuned to regional politics and personalities. Local matchmakers need to develop expertise about the businesses and nonprofits in their regions, their issues, leadership, culture, community dynamics, and key players.

The Bottom Line

The nonprofit sector faces serious strategic and financial challenges, yet each organization has unique and often complex circumstances. The key is to help each organization assess and articulate the assistance it needs and then to refer candidates who bring the necessary expertise as well as a passion for the mission. An effective matchmaker is a key factor in helping a board engage qualified new members as well as volunteer consultants. Properly matched board candidates and management-assistance volunteers can advance a nonprofit organization in the face of dynamic challenges and opportunities. Furthermore, the volunteers derive a sense of purpose and achievement from their work. Most important, the community benefits by having healthy nonprofits that provide vital community services.

The value of involving people with business skills in assisting nonprofit organizations will be more fully realized if board candidates and volunteer consultants are prepared for the distinctive issues facing nonprofits. There are important differences between the for-profit and nonprofit revenue models and organizational cultures. Businesspeople who work with nonprofits can maximize their effectiveness by seeking training, guidance, and coaching in order to learn how to make the transition to the nonprofit environment. Nonprofit organizations need regional resource centers that they can count on for high-quality board-matching and training services. With good matching services, nonprofits can leverage good will for the benefit of the community.

4

Making the Translation from the Business World to the Nonprofit World

We could declare each other products of different cultures—as we, of course, are—and leave it, respectfully, at that. But that would leave us separate and impermeable—something that is easier to accept with impersonal entities like class, or gender, or country than with a fellow human being clamoring to be understood. . . . A true translation proceeds by the motions of understanding and sympathy; it happens by slow increments, sentence-by-sentence, phrase-by-phrase.

—Eva Hoffman, Lost in Translation, *1989*

Picture thousands of business executives and professionals channeled onto nonprofit boards of directors. Imagine that their involvement has been carefully facilitated by matching their personal interests and qualifications to the nonprofits that need strategic expertise to meet today's challenges. Consider the range of experience these board candidates might bring—in the areas of law, human resources, public relations, strategic planning, marketing, pricing, fundraising, real estate, finance, accounting, information systems, and so on. Imagine further that each business executive and professional chooses only one or two boards where he or she feels a personal passion for and commitment to the mission. It would be powerful, transformative.

Although it is inspiring to envision nonprofit boards bolstered by people with business skills, there are hazards as well. Nonprofits can attest to the troublesome dynamics that can be created by well-meaning businesspeople who have accidentally stirred up trouble rather than providing constructive assistance. The potential win-win for the board member and the nonprofit can quickly wither; the volunteer can be frustrated, the nonprofit worse off than it was, and the volunteer's employer embarrassed and missing an opportunity to engage. As William Bowen, president of the Rockefeller Foundation, has noted, "For some people from the for-profit sector, joining nonprofit boards involves venturing into unknown territory. The boards of nonprofit organizations may include individuals who, while highly competent in some general sense, fail to understand how a ballet company functions or how graduate education relates to undergraduate education. Board members with no visceral feel for an organization may bring values to the board table that are simply inappropriate" (1994, p. 5).

Although businesspeople have valuable talents to offer, they are entering a new realm, with its own culture, language, and challenges, when they volunteer on a nonprofit board. Businesspeople need to approach this new role with openness and humility, be prepared to learn, and then figure out how to use their business skills to advance the organization. "It is critically important that the most able people in the business world make the considerable effort necessary to function effectively in what may seem to be a strange realm—one in which missions are sometimes difficult to define with precision, resources are almost always scarce, and relevant data and analyses are either unavailable or slippery to the touch" (Bowen, 1994, p. 6).

Making the translation is a two-way street. In order to leverage the value of business volunteers, nonprofit executives need to open themselves to new perspectives that might seem alien at first.

Businesspeople may bring a market-oriented view that requires nonprofit executives to think and communicate in new ways about mission, organizational focus and results, and revenue models. Nonprofit executives need to translate their perspective into a language businesspeople can understand. By listening to each other, business volunteers and nonprofit staffs can work together to strengthen organizations in serving the community and building additional support. For example, businesspeople need to understand the complexities of measurement in the nonprofit world, while nonprofit executives need to improve measurement systems and reports. Additionally, businesspeople need to realize the importance of the consensus-building process, while nonprofit executives need to accelerate organizational decision making.

The strangeness of the nonprofit environment to business volunteers is revealed by data. Based on a 45 percent response rate of 173 board members placed by a matchmaker (a number of whom were placed on more than one board) in 2002 and 2003, 44 percent indicated that they felt that the "organization's challenges were more complex than anticipated" (*BVU Survey of Board Candidates Elected Through BVU, 2002–2003*). These board members were all in executive positions at businesses, many had MBA degrees, and many had consulted to dozens of large and small corporations. As Weld Royal observed in the *New York Times:* "Serving on [nonprofit] boards can bolster [the] . . . careers [of businesspeople] by putting them in touch with well-connected individuals and giving their companies a good name. It also lets them use their management expertise for the good of society. That much the executives expect. What many don't anticipate, however, is how frustrating the work can be" (Royal, 2002, p. 12).

In spite of the challenges, nonprofits that engage volunteers in productive board service can benefit. Furthermore, successful board members will revel in the good feelings that come from helping others and improving lives in the community; the profits are not financial, they are humanistic and spiritual. In the survey noted above,

83 percent of executives felt they "made a useful contribution" to their nonprofit boards, and 80 percent felt "their contribution was valued." Seventy-five percent had a "mostly rewarding experience." Only 9 percent had a "frustrating board experience." Note that each of these board members had been placed on a board through a one-on-one matching process and all had participated in a minimum of three hours of board training; these factors are likely to have increased the chances of the experiences being rewarding, rather than frustrating.

Key Elements in Making the Translation

A careful look at effective volunteer-nonprofit relationships reveals the following key factors in their success:

Board Members Should Have a Personal Passion for the Mission of the Nonprofit

Traditionally, nonprofit board members have been identified and engaged rather randomly. People are often invited to serve by their friends and colleagues for social or business reasons. In these cases, the new board member may not connect with the mission. However, in today's challenging environment, new board members are likely to be called on to provide serious amounts of time and money. Unless they are truly excited about the cause, they and the nonprofit are likely to be disappointed.

Some volunteers choose organizations that address illnesses and diseases that have touched their lives or the lives of loved ones. Others choose boards that address issues of inclusion in order to help integrate diverse people into the community. Yet others focus their efforts on issues of domestic violence, education, and services for seniors. Successful board members derive their energy from a belief in the compelling value of the organization. Board participation and charity are, after all, purely voluntary activities. Passion (and possibly a little peer pressure) is the only motivation for optimal performance.

The board members who have the most positive experiences are the ones who raise their hands and offer to help. The individuals who took part in the survey referenced above had successful experiences because they chose where they would engage based on their interests, and they participated at a meaningful level: 57 percent had risen to board leadership positions. Of those, 91 percent indicated that they would "serve again" in a leadership role; 95 percent encouraged others to serve on nonprofit boards.

When volunteers have a visceral connection to the work of an organization, or a true conviction about the value of the nonprofit's mission and services, they will have the patience and commitment to overcome obstacles. They will learn what they need to know and will engage in the process. They will also gain the respect of others because no one is as compelling, persuasive, and charismatic as a true believer. Thus, it is important for nonprofits to ascertain a board candidate's true interests in order to ensure that the organization fits within the individual's personal agenda.

Volunteers Should Respect the Difference between Mission-Related and Profit-Oriented Organizations

Successful board members understand that the staff and volunteers of nonprofits are motivated primarily by their passion for the mission, not by a desire to make money. By appreciating this difference between motivation in nonprofits and for-profits, businesspeople on boards will understand the necessity of achieving consensus whenever possible in order to accomplish organizational goals. Key stakeholders who are part of the decision-making process and are engaged and supportive of major strategic directions will stop at nothing to help achieve success. People whose input is ignored will be alienated.

Professor Andrew Morriss of Case Western Reserve University School of Law, with a Ph.D. in economics from MIT, points out that because money is not a motivating force for nonprofit boards and volunteers (and is usually not a motivator for nonprofit staff members either), there are only two possible rewards—psychic rewards and prestige (interview, April 21, 2004). In order to motivate volunteers, organizations must ensure that they derive psychic satisfaction and, in some cases, receive public recognition. Business leaders are also cognizant of the cost of failing in the public eye. For many people, such motivation can be more powerful than financial gain.

By understanding the motivating forces and reward systems for volunteers, nonprofits can help board members make the translation into the nonprofit realm. This understanding of volunteers' motivations has implications for planning processes, decision making, and recognition. For example, the failure to thank an employee at a for-profit might simply annoy the person. The failure to give proper thanks to volunteers, however, can potentially alienate valuable people who constitute vital human capital to the nonprofit.

Board Members Should Understand the Financial Model and Board Culture of the Nonprofit

Many nonprofits have complex revenue models to support the various services they provide; this is often one of the most difficult areas for businesspeople to comprehend. Steve Chapin's experience moving from the for-profit to the nonprofit sector as a financial officer is instructive (interview, June 28, 2004). After serving for sixteen years as the controller and information-technology manager of Lesco, a company with annual sales of $175 million that produces chemicals and fertilizers for colleges and golf courses, Chapin joined the Achievement Centers for Children as its director of finance and operations. The Achievement Centers for Children is a $3 million nonprofit that serves children with special needs and their families. Like most businesspeople, Chapin thought it would be easy to manage a far smaller budget than he had been used to. Chapin came from a business with a typical revenue model that revolved around a logical pricing strategy and a set of customers who paid the company directly. In his new nonprofit position, Chapin found himself juggling thirty-five different cost centers, such as occupational, physical, and speech therapy; day care; a summer camp; autism classes;

technical assessments; and training and placement services. Each of these programs is funded through complex payer mixes including Medicaid, preferred provider organizations (PPOs), health management organizations (HMOs), foundation grants, endowment interest, private philanthropy, and fees for services. Each funding source has its own reporting systems and payout schedules. In addition, several accrediting organizations have their own compliance requirements, and it is necessary to be accredited in order to receive funding. Clients are served regardless of their ability to pay, and the agency must manage increasing costs without the opportunity to raise its prices because prices are dictated by Medicaid, the HMOs, and the PPOs. Chapin describes his job as "walking a high wire between costs and fees."

His advice to businesspeople joining nonprofit boards is to understand that a nonprofit is not at all like a for-profit business and to "listen to the staff who are highly experienced." In spite of the challenges, Chapin adds that he absolutely "loves" working at the agency. Why? "For what we do . . . and for Pat," referring to Patricia Nobili, the president and CEO of the Achievement Centers for Children. "I have never had a better boss." These are the psychic rewards that are key incentives to nonprofit staff members.

In addition to understanding the difference in financial models, board members need to realize that comparisons with for-profit boards are of limited value. For-profit board members are compensated (an incentive to prepare for and attend meetings); they are accountable to stakeholders (which is clearly measurable through stock values); and the CEO is often chair of the board.

Board Members Must Understand the Complexities of Measuring Success

Businesses determine success and failure by clear measures of profit and loss, return on investment, and change in shareholder value. For nonprofit organizations, however, measures of success are often complex and elusive. For example, how would an organization that serves urban, poor children determine the number of young people who will not succumb to drugs or gangs from the ages of ten to eighteen because they participated in a particular after-school mentoring and tutoring program when they were eight to twelve years old? How would one demonstrate that involving children in grades 3 through 5 in weekend arts and music classes will enrich their lives and increase their likelihood for success in school and careers? Longitudinal studies, which examine outcomes over many years or even decades, are costly because they require multiyear funding for salaries for experienced researchers and information-tracking systems. Furthermore, even if it could be shown that over the course of a decade the majority of children who participated in these particular programs did in fact "achieve success," how could it be shown that these particular programs were the key factor? After all, other influencing factors could distort the results; correlation is not causation. Perhaps the parents of these children were more engaged in parenting, for example, and this was the key factor rather than the after-school program.

Even if a longitudinal study could show that a service was useful, is the high cost of such research more valuable than funding the service itself? At what point can reasonable people decide that it is more beneficial for poor, urban children to go to an after-school program for tutoring, mentoring, or art classes than to go home to empty houses while their parents work or to play on the streets in neighborhoods that are dominated by gangs?

Other examples of programs whose ultimate outcomes are difficult and costly although not impossible to measure include the following:

- The impact of environmental education provided by a botanical garden center. To what extent will people be influenced in their personal lives and business decisions after they participate?

- The impact of a board consulting service. Is success
  measured by an increase in the client organization's
  budget? a decrease in the budget that shows increased
  efficiency? improved attendance rates at board meetings? a merger with another organization? the departure
  of the chief executive? the departure of several board
  members?

- The value of having a first-class symphony orchestra.
  Is success measured by ticket sales? How does the
  symphony play an educational role? How does it
  expand people's horizons?

- The value of providing hospice care to those who are
  dying and their families. Is success measured by the
  rate of referrals from hospitals and medical personnel?
  by feedback from families?

Keeping in mind the challenges and costs of evaluation and
assessment, board members should nonetheless ask two important
questions: How will we know that the organization is accomplish-
ing what it has set out to do? How will we know that the organization's finite resources have the highest possible impact? Balancing
the need for useful information with the costs of evaluation, boards
should expect the staff to seek ways to evaluate each core program's
effectiveness and benchmark the results against those for related
programs in other communities. In the after-school example above,
the board might benefit from hearing a presentation from a best-
practices expert in the field who can compare the local programming to other cities' programs; the board might also want to see
quarterly data regarding the number of children in the program, the
cost of serving each child, the goals of the services, and some kind
of assessment of the extent to which goals are met. The assessment
can include comments from children who participate in response

to the question: Why do you come here after school or on weekends? Do you think your friends should come too? If you didn't come here, what would you do instead? What do you most like about coming here? What do you see or do that you never did before? Interviews and focus groups with parents and perhaps with the daytime school-teachers of these children might also provide insights. For example, improvements in grades, decreases in drug use, and fewer or no court appearances could indicate positive results.

Board members are not the only ones who need to adjust their thinking about measurement when they enter the nonprofit environment. The chief executives and staff members of nonprofit organizations must also rethink their attitudes about assessment. Too often, nonprofit staffs have claimed that best practices in business, including measurement, have no place in the nonprofit sector. Contrary to such thinking, nonprofits can learn from the for-profit sector how to assess the cost and value of services and to align revenues accordingly. Furthermore, nonprofit staff members must understand that the best way to attract and build resources for good causes is to demonstrate the value, benefits, and impact of nonprofit services. Those who invest time and resources expect information that demonstrates that their commitment is in fact useful. In addition, organizational supporters—board members, funders, volunteers, and even paid staff members themselves—need to see how their dollars and time are being invested. For example, which programs and services yield the greatest results for the people who are served by the agency?

The staff therefore needs to find a way to capture the value of programs and services so that the board and funders can have confidence in the benefits of supporting the services. Essentially, the board and funders need to consider the cost-benefit analysis of various modes of information gathering, and the staff should be creative and forthcoming in seeking ways to capture the value in a presentable fashion.

Additionally, nonprofits should keep in mind that measurement is necessary for ongoing organizational planning. Only by tracking and monitoring progress can the staff members determine how best to focus their efforts and improve services for clients and the community. Useful information can be gathered about the number of clients served, the hours of service provided, and the number of clients who refer others. Focus groups and surveys can yield additional information for assessing the quality of services. The chief executive is responsible for developing measurement systems and reports, and the board's role is to hold the chief executive accountable.

Measurement is an area where businesspeople can add significant value by raising questions and assisting in developing a report format that tells the board how the organization is doing. Reports of organizational impact strengthen the case for support and also facilitate good organizational decision making.

Board Members Should be Thoughtful about Board Process and Ask Questions

Once new board members understand how the organization operates, they can begin to formulate ideas for improvements and perhaps even engage others in fostering progress. Board members who sit by passively are not serving the organization or the community. Nonprofits should expect their board members to be attentive and to ask questions that will help illuminate challenges as well as opportunities. The purpose of asking questions is not for board members to show off their intellect but rather to illuminate a weakness or threat that needs attention. By asking questions, board members accelerate their own learning and, additionally, are likely to help others on the board to ask questions too.

Often new board members who have business experience realize that the board they have joined is not fully engaged and focused on the higher-level issues of organizational purpose and direction and that the board is becoming involved in the operational matters that are the responsibility of the chief executive. A few apparent symptoms of board distress might be lack of attendance at board meetings; meeting agendas or discussions that are not concentrated on the most important organizational issues and that instead delve into narrow management issues; or lack of adequate board involvement in contributing or raising funds.

A new board member can sometimes stimulate new thinking simply by asking good questions. These questions need not necessarily be asked in the board meeting; they can be posed first in a one-on-one conversation with the chief executive and possibly with the board chair. The new board member can then gradually and cautiously engage a few other board members in conversation about the organization. It is important for the new board member to ask the following questions: Will my ideas for change truly advance the mission and the organization? What is the potential for added value? What might the negative fall-out be, and how can the negative repercussions be mitigated? What is the best process for engaging others?

All these issues regarding process fundamentally pertain to consensus building. Building consensus to make decisions can be confusing and frustrating for business volunteers. Not everyone has the stamina to endure such cumbersome processes in order to advance the organization. The process, however absurd to business volunteers, is nonetheless essential. Because nonprofit boards, staffs, and volunteers are motivated by their devotion to the mission of the organization rather than by financial benefit, their agreement on an organization's mission, structure, and future is important. Decisions that alienate key stakeholders will cost the organization important support, and so it is worth the investment of time to achieve consensus whenever possible. At the same time, as discussed in Chapter Six, board leaders need to sustain a satisfactory pace and momentum to ensure that decisions are made on a timely basis.

The importance of process cannot be overstated. A reckless process will be destructive. A thoughtful process can advance the organization and help new board members make the translation into the nonprofit culture.

Boards Need to Assess the Skills, Experiences, and Relationships of Their Members

Nonprofits should be purposeful in choosing whom to invite onto the board, and candidates should also be particular about the organizations they join. Nonprofits should only invite board members who are willing to bring expertise and make introductions to people and organizations whose support and influence can be useful. Board members should think deliberately about how they can be helpful. Furthermore, they should be generous in sharing their time and expertise as well as providing financial support.

Board members need not be connected to the world's most powerful people in order to generate significant financial resources. Often an important funder can be persuaded to support an organization based on a passionate request from a devoted board member. Even more ambitious board members can imagine extraordinary ways to support the organization. When one small-business owner joined the board of a large health care foundation in the Midwest, no one could have imagined that he would engage former New York City mayor Rudolph Giuliani to be the main speaker at the annual fundraising event. The board member did not know Giuliani, but he met someone on a plane who did know him, and the board member's passion and persistence persuaded Giuliani to speak. The event attracted seven hundred guests and raised $940,000, more than quadruple the amount raised at any event sponsored by the foundation in prior years.

Board Members Should Always Expect Excellence

Board members should encourage superior standards and be proactive in helping the entire organization to achieve excellence. The board is entrusted with charitable and public funding; its job is to ensure that the community is served well. When nonprofits under-perform, their boards are responsible.

Businesspeople can have insights into and suggest ways to as-sess organizational excellence and to track performance. For exam-ple, they can bring expertise regarding hiring and retention practices that will help the board to engage and support a qualified chief executive. Businesspeople can also help the chief executive develop measures for monitoring and documenting progress.

Board Members Should Learn from Those Who Are Experienced

Serving on a board can be a powerful learning experience. Board members can develop their skills in consensus building, group dynamics, and leadership. They can contribute effectively and become leaders by observing how others attain respect and earn the authority and power to lead. In fact, businesspeople see a connec-tion between their nonprofit and for-profit governance experiences. Leslie Rahl, president and CEO, Capital Market Risk Advisors, New York, observed that "I have served on many nonprofit boards, but it was only last year, when I joined the Fannie Mae board (my first for-profit board), that I realized the value of my nonprofit ex-perience in being chosen for a for-profit board, and the value of board training, which I received at Harvard Business School" (inter-view, January 24, 2005).

Board Members Should Recognize Achievements

Success is never achieved by accident. Each and every organiza-tional victory is the result of the hard work of the board and staff members. It is important to celebrate victories and to recognize everyone's efforts and achievements. Recognition reinforces those who contribute and also sets an example for others. It is a good idea to start every board meeting with comments about new successes and thanks to each key person who helped achieve them.

Board members should realize that the chief executive probably works tirelessly for the organization, and they should be sure to recognize those efforts as well. According to CompassPoint in San Francisco, one of the nation's leading nonprofit resource centers, "The most significant challenges of the executive role are high stress and long hours, anxiety about finances, fundraising, and managing people" (Masaoka, 2003, pp. 82–83). By recognizing and appreciating the chief executive, the board can provide much-needed support.

Board Members Should Always Think about the Organization's Mission

The mission should be like a Times Square neon sign in the mind of everyone involved. The mission drives energy, enthusiasm, and progress. The mission should be stated on meeting agendas and organizational materials as a constant reminder. When conflicts arise, the organization should seek consensus by reminding itself of the mission. When opportunities arise, the organization should seek its inspiration from the mission. Nonprofits receive tax-exempt status in return for providing value to the community. Nonprofit boards must adhere to the fiduciary duty of obedience—obedience to the mission—and all decisions of the board must be oriented toward achieving it.

The Chief Executive as Facilitator of the Transition to the Nonprofit Culture

The nonprofit executive plays an important role in engaging board members by facilitating their transition into the nonprofit sector. The chief executive should become acquainted with all board members to find out what has drawn them to the board and how their expertise, relationships, and passion can become assets for the organization and its mission.

Given that the nonprofit sector is complex, one of the initial limitations is board members' lack of knowledge about operations and context. Board members should be chosen for their strategic acumen and their commitment to the mission, but they rarely have the background necessary for making key organizational decisions. The chief executive needs to strengthen the board by sharing essential expertise, vision, and supporting data. The chief executive must provide succinct and compelling information regarding the needs of the community, the organizational services that are addressing those needs, and, most important, the context in which the nonprofit organization is functioning.

The executive needs to choose useful formats for providing information so that the board can digest it. Board members should be provided with an orientation at the outset of their involvement as well as ongoing information. Even those who have experience on other boards need to be reminded about their fiduciary responsibilities, and all new board members need clear information about the organization, its purpose, its vision and strategic direction, its revenue model, and its financial situation. Board members need a copy of the by-laws, a list of board members, outlines of board committees, financial information, and a summary of the nonprofit's strategic vision. Information for board-member orientations as well as ongoing communication with the board can be provided in written and electronic form, at educational forums designed for the board, and through participation in local, regional, or national meetings.

Too many nonprofit organizations are stalled because the board lacks the information it needs to make strategic decisions. One multi-million-dollar social services organization in New York that is experiencing spiraling deficits has a board comprising business executives who have absolutely no awareness of the revenue model. None of them has the time to understand the organization's financial affairs, although they are being asked for hefty financial contributions to help fill large budget gaps. Even worse, the chief executive is unable to provide a map of the key revenue sources, the risks, and the opportunities. Without a capable chief executive, there is no hope for this organization. The losers are the members of the community who need the vital services it provides.

An effective nonprofit executive provides the board with concise and relevant information, focuses the board on the organization's strategic issues, establishes measures that help the board understand the relative value and importance of each core program, and engages the board in meaningful discussions of organizational matters. By being well-informed, board members are able to contribute to board decision making in ways that best serve the community's interests.

On Nonprofits Being More Businesslike

Businesspeople and funders often believe that nonprofits should be more "businesslike." But it is important to be clear when applying this term to nonprofits. Without clarity, a businessperson serving on a nonprofit board might assume that being businesslike automatically means cutting services that are difficult to fund, providing incentives by allowing employees to share in year-end financial surpluses, selling lucrative advertising space to companies whose interests are contrary to the mission of the organization (such as beer ads in the promotional material of an alcoholism-recovery organization), or merging with another nonprofit whose mission is not appropriate (such as a domestic-violence center merging with a housing facility for men). Such suggestions from businesspeople on nonprofit boards not only undermine the organizations' effectiveness but also breed misunderstanding between the board and the staff. To prevent a deteriorating situation, nonprofit staff members need to be open to business practices that are suitable and useful, while businesspeople on boards need to understand what is not suitable.

What Businesslike Should Not Mean

Decisions made in business are ultimately designed to increase profits. Decisions in the nonprofit sector are designed to increase value in serving the community. Businesspeople must understand the implications of this very fundamental difference in objectives.

Making Decisions to Continue Services Based on Their Profitability

Mission and sustainability, not profitability, should be the keys in deciding about the continuation of particular services in a nonprofit organization. Nonprofits are tax-exempt and are funded by charitable gifts and government dollars because they meet community needs that are not met through the free-market, for-profit sector.

According to F. Warren McFarlan, "In business, when a unit is in financial trouble you either fix it, sell it, or shut it down. For the nonprofit organization, however, a loss-making unit may be at the center of the group's mission and its raison d'etre" (1999, p. 68). It is therefore incumbent on the board to be inventive and ambitious in seeking revenue sources for the services that are most relevant to the mission. They may even need to seek organizational mergers in order to ensure the long-term viability of much-needed services. Unlike businesses, however, they do not have the option of simply cutting programs that lose money.

Remember that if a homeless shelter could be "profitable," it would be a hotel. If a hunger center could be "profitable," it would be a restaurant. Nonprofits often serve people in need, so these organizations are dependent on charity to meet their missions. A shelter that "loses money" is not "poorly managed."

Making Top-Down Decisions Without the Input of Key Constituencies

Ultimately, the board and the chief executive of a nonprofit may have to make some unpopular decisions. Because nonprofits depend so much on community and funder good will, however, it is important to include the input of key constituents in the decision-making process. Constituents include funders, board members, volunteers, staff, clients, and sometimes public officials. This procedure can be cumbersome at times, but shortcuts can undermine the organization in the longer term. For-profit businesses usually have more latitude than nonprofits to act rapidly and independently.

What Businesslike Should Mean

Although there are fundamental differences in the business and nonprofit sectors in terms of mission, purpose, and process, at the same time there are practices that are useful in both environments. Nonprofits can elevate their performance by adopting certain business practices.

Taking Board Governance Seriously

In comparing nonprofit boards to for-profit boards, experts who serve on both types comment on the need for nonprofit board members to take their governance roles seriously. Vartan Gregorian, president of the Carnegie Corporation Foundation, says that nonprofit board members need to "attend *in* meetings, not *at* meetings, and to give the same time and respect that they give to for-profit boards" (interview, 2004).

Focusing in Laserlike Fashion on the Key Issues

It is common, and absurd, for nonprofit boards to waste countless hours deliberating about minor operating issues while avoiding serious discussion of the most significant challenges and opportunities. One of the greatest skills that many businesspeople can bring to nonprofits is the ability to size up the situation and focus attention on the issues that matter most. For example, the board should not spend time making hiring decisions about staff members (other than the chief executive), reviewing highly detailed budgets, or planning the color scheme at the annual luncheon. The board should be focused on potential revenue gaps and how they can be filled, the programs and services that are the most important to sustain, and strategic alliances that might ensure the longer-term viability of key services. The board should concern itself with impending legislation that will jeopardize funding for key programs or force the organization to make fundamental changes in the delivery of services. The chief executive and the board chair should alert the board to major issues, provide information that will support decision making, and focus meeting agendas on these key matters. Board members with business acumen can help the board stay focused.

Establishing a Viable Revenue Model

Although many who staff nonprofit organizations feel the urge to meet the vast and compelling needs of their clients, an organization is sustainable only if it can generate the necessary resources. Unfortunately, a lack of resources often means limiting services. For example, in order to achieve its primary mission, a welfare-to-work organization might need to narrow its focus to job training and job placement, and forgo programs that broaden the career horizons of teenagers. In other cases, in order to align revenues and expenses, the organization might need to adopt a sliding scale, fee-for-service model. For example, a program that teaches illiterate adults to read might charge employers a suitable fee, while providing its services to low-income clients at a discount, and free to homeless people. A nonprofit consulting service might charge full fees to larger organizations with budgets in the tens of millions, while offering its consulting services to smaller organizations at a heavily discounted rate.

Strategic plans without realistic budgets are meaningless. At the end of the day, the organization must assess the costs of providing services, take stock of its revenues, and determine what is possible and what is not. Each nonprofit needs to construct a revenue model, a plan to generate a mix of revenue streams that will support the programs and services offered. Businesspeople on boards can help explore new revenue opportunities and make sure that the organization has carefully and thoughtfully aligned revenues and expenses.

Having the Courage to Make Decisions, and Basing Them on Relevant Information.

Nonprofits need to define the challenge or opportunity, outline the options and the respective pros and cons, gather data and information, and then decide. All constituents may not be pleased, but choices do need to be made based on a rational process. Decisions that will affect the viability of the organization and its success in serving the community should not be based on emotions, but rather on a methodical and reasonable analysis of various courses of action. Passion should drive energy, but decisions should be based on reality. Conflicts between emotions and rationality often occur when the "old guard" is reluctant to address current needs and interests. At such times, the board chair and chief executive need to lead an inclusive process and then have the courage to advance new approaches. Sometimes, outside facilitators can be helpful.

Making the Case for the Organization

Nonprofits may excel at serving their clients, but they are often remiss in communicating to key stakeholders the compelling value of their services, broadening their base of support, and making a clear case for funding. Nonprofits need to use good business practices to promote their work and build support.

Engaging, Compensating Appropriately, and Supporting Outstanding Chief Executives and Senior Staff People

The time has come for the nonprofit sector to take the position of chief executive seriously. As shown earlier, the challenges facing nonprofits are highly complex. Traditionally, chief executives of nonprofits receive limited compensation packages. For example, the typical salary for the chief executive of a nonprofit organization with a budget of $1 to $4.9 million is $50,000 to $75,000 (*The Nonprofit Governance Index,* 2000, p. 9). Despite low compensation, chief executives need to have extensive experience in finance, grants, human resource management, program management, and marketing and communications. They often work over fifty hours a week and usually do not have a full complement of senior staff members with extensive experience in accounting, human resources, and fundraising and so often handle many of these jobs themselves. It is rare to attract and retain a well-qualified person for this kind of position.

Nonprofit boards must realize that if they want organizations to be well run, they need to engage highly qualified people, compensate them appropriately, and then support them in leading the organization. The board's role is to provide oversight and support, not to run the organization. In addition, according to an auditor who works with dozens of nonprofits of all sizes, ultimately, nonprofits will need to merge in order to become large enough and to have sufficient resources to engage well-qualified senior staff members including first-rate chief financial officers (interview, Donna Sciarappa, May 25, 2004). This is another issue nonprofit boards need to contemplate and explore.

National Organizations

The boards and staff of the local affiliates and chapters of national organizations have a particular advantage in accessing resources and information regarding the broader nonprofit context, as well as information on innovations and best (and failed) practices. An outstanding national conference, for example, was held by the Make A Wish Foundation in November 2003. It was special for two reasons. First, the conference was designed specifically for pairs of board chairs and chief executives of the affiliates rather than staff only; the national chair, Suzanne Sutter, president and chief executive officer of Things Remembered, a national chain of gift stores with annual sales of more than $270 million, personally encouraged the chairs of

affiliates to attend. This conference design underscored and supported the relationship between the chair and the executive.

Second, the organization created a highly concentrated program agenda with a purpose and a method. Sutter worked with the
chief executive to design a two-day agenda that encouraged the affiliates to set ambitious goals, learn what they needed to achieve
such goals, and clearly distinguish between the role of board chairs,
chief executives, and board members. Sutter engaged volunteers
from McKinsey & Company to help her and the staff prepare for
the conference by gathering information about the performance
of the national and affiliate offices, the potential for increased success, and the specific steps for setting ambitious goals.

The conference began with an overview of the McKinsey report.
Then, the conference provided training for the leadership teams of
the affiliates. In a number of sessions, the most successful affiliates
were featured; they described particular approaches that could be
adopted by struggling affiliates. The conference was orchestrated to
facilitate change by defining the desired outcomes and providing
tools and methods for measurable results. People left the conference
inspired and energized with a clear road map of exactly what to do
next in order to further advance a cause in which they truly believed. The conference helped the local affiliates to increase their
understanding of purposes, goals, and specific and practical approaches to achieve success.

In 2004, the national Make A Wish Foundation (MAWF) board
engaged its chapters in redesigning the national governance structure. In 2005, with a new model and charter, the national board
committed itself to a new strategic direction to increase the value
of the national office in providing supportive services to strengthen
MAWF and its chapters nationwide. This is an example of a national board, composed of businesspeople and philanthropists,
leveraging the national brand and relationships to advance the mission to "grant the wishes of children with life-threatening medical

conditions to enrich the human experience with hope, strength, and joy" (interview, Suzanne Sutter, January 22, 2005).

National organizations that are attentive to the challenges and opportunities facing their affiliates can provide vital assistance by teaching successful practices, providing back office and shared services (such as accounting, finance, health care benefits, human resources, communications, and fundraising), and enhancing the brand image and fundraising potential. There will be less waste on trial and error among a large group of similar organizations if there is a communications system to facilitate learning and disseminate best practices.

Advice from an Experienced Nonprofit Board Member

"We don't even know what we don't know," says Eugene Lang, founder and chairman emeritus of the "I Have A Dream" Foundation (interview, 2004), and the "we" refers to businesspeople who become involved in the nonprofit sector. Lang has useful lessons to share with businesspeople who are entering the nonprofit realm. Following an extraordinarily successful international business career that lasted for over forty years, Lang has devoted himself to what is now more than two decades of improving the lives of public school children from the poorest urban communities. Through his immersion in the nonprofit sector, he has developed an appreciation for the distinctions between for-profit and nonprofit enterprises.

In 1981, Lang promised the graduating class of an elementary school in Harlem that he would pay for the college education of each student in the class. This was the beginning of a long, challenging, and rewarding period in his life. With his background as a highly successful international entrepreneur who himself went to college on a full scholarship at the age of fifteen (Swarthmore, Class of 1938) and who has thirty honorary college degrees from the nation's most prominent colleges and universities, one might imagine that Lang could figure out solutions to improve public education. But as he tells it, his first lesson was that he didn't even know what he didn't know. He entered into this project with all good intentions, but it took him three years to establish honest and open communications with the students in the class he adopted. Lang educated himself by spending time with the students every week of the school year. He learned by listening. Twenty-three years later, Mr. Lang has inspired and guided other philanthropists nationwide to sponsor young students' college educations.

Lang cautions that "business success does not give you the capacity to deal with social issues." He explains that basic principles of business and economics do not directly apply to the education of children. "Educating children is not the same as producing automobiles," he says. Lang's advice to businesspeople is to "understand what you do not know." Furthermore, Lang cautions that a businessperson cannot presume to learn and understand the nonprofit environment in a few hours a month; he encourages businesspeople on boards to pay attention to the experts who are immersed in the nonprofit sector and the particular service area. He also notes that, in many cases, the greatest support businesspeople can give to nonprofits is to write checks and lend their names for credibility.

Businesspeople who seek to make a meaningful contribution in helping nonprofits to achieve success can learn valuable lessons from Lang. Most important, the first step is realizing what you do not know and what it will take to increase your understanding of the unique circumstances of the nonprofit sector.

The Bottom Line

Businesspeople will make valuable contributions to nonprofits, develop themselves in the process, and probably even have some fun only by appreciating the uniqueness of the sector, the specific cause they have chosen, and their role as board members.

A nonprofit can leverage the skills of businesspeople only when business volunteers take the time and effort to learn about the nonprofit and its particular circumstances. Volunteers can add value when they join nonprofits with humility and a willingness to learn.

5

Understanding What It Means
to Govern

Whatever you can do or dream you can, begin it.
Boldness has genius, power and magic in it.
Begin it now.

— *Johann Wolfgang von Goethe*, Faust, *1835*

All nonprofit boards have a basic set of roles and responsibilities. In addition, each board must have a thoughtful discussion at least annually about its big agenda for taking the organization forward. Every nonprofit has several key matters that, if attended to, can improve its service to the community. Furthermore, all board members must commit themselves to support the organization. Without such clarity and determination on the part of the board, nonprofits blow in the wind and succumb to random forces. In order to achieve success, a board must work in concert with the chief executive. Together, their job is to establish a compelling mission and vision based on clearly documented community interests, develop and implement high-impact programs and services, create contemporary and effective revenue models, and document and report program results.

In an era when the viability of nonprofits is in jeopardy, many boards are complacent, trapped in an outdated paradigm. Too many board members continue to recruit individuals merely because they are acquaintances, expand the board beyond a reasonable working size to retain members whose involvement is no longer meaningful, maintain obsolete committees, and, worst of all, drone on in dull meetings that have little if anything to do with the most pressing organizational issues. Not only does this outmoded model fail to address the most important strategic issues, but it also discourages participation by people who would be valuable. Busy business executives and professionals who can bring much-needed expertise to the boardroom spurn board involvement that is aimless or perfunctory.

Moreover, nonprofit boards have legal and fiduciary responsibilities, including the duties of care, loyalty, and obedience. The duty of care requires that board members attend meetings, read and prepare for meetings, and be informed. The duty of care includes the business judgment rule, which allows for bad decisions as long as the board can show that it conducted its work with care, attention, and good faith. The duty of loyalty requires that board members put service to the nonprofit organization above their personal and professional interests. When conflicts of interest occur, board members must inform the board so that it can decide whether to excuse the board member from related decisions or from membership on the board altogether. The duty of obedience is the beauty of nonprofit organizations. It requires that all board decisions be driven by the organization's mission (Leifer and Glomb, 1997).

The pressure on boards to improve is driven by public calls for transparency and accountability, especially in organizations that rely on charitable and public funding. Media attention to institutional integrity is revealing organizational and governance flaws; when organizations stumble or fail, boards are being held accountable. The bar has been raised for board performance by the Sarbanes-Oxley Act of 2002. Although Sarbanes-Oxley was written for for-profits, aspects of the legislation have become the gold standard for nonprofits as well, especially with regard to financial oversight by boards of directors. Thus, boards must reform themselves to meet their legal and moral responsibilities. Moreover, only high-functioning boards can leverage the energy and talents of business-people to advance their missions.

Boards that are in distress need to establish a clear and logical system for effective governance. Described in this chapter are steps a board can take to affirm its roles and responsibilities, focus on the key strategic challenges and opportunities facing the organization, and establish standards and procedures for accountability. The next chapter describes a process for realigning the board structure and composition so that it can effectively address contemporary issues.

Understanding and Accepting the Role of the Board

The first step in improving the board's effectiveness is to clarify its role. Traditionally, board members figured out their role by watching others; and, as a result, bad habits have been passed down. Today, a growing body of literature and materials, as well as training, can help boards understand their roles. Boards should have an annual discussion about their role and follow basic guidelines regarding their domain. The key activities described in this section must be performed by every board.

Hiring, Evaluating, and Supporting the Chief Executive

The single most important activity a board undertakes is hiring a chief executive because the chief executive plays the most significant role in achieving organizational effectiveness. Organizations succeed or fail depending on the chief executive. Unfortunately, examples abound of nonprofits that are stagnant or failing because they do not have a professional leader. Even though foundations may suggest and fund the formulation of a strategic plan for an organization, without strong executive leadership, such a plan is meaningless. Furthermore, board members cannot fill the gap when an organization does not have a dedicated and experienced executive.

In hiring mode, boards need to consider the potential of their organizations, the skills and qualifications that will be required of chief executives, and an appropriate compensation package. Once they have hired their chief executives, boards need to help them be effective by introducing them to key people in the community, complimenting and recognizing them when appropriate, and providing constructive support, advice, and assistance. Boards should respect chief executives as leaders, as the people with the greatest expertise, as the individuals most fully immersed in their organizations, as spokespeople, and as the people most invested in organizational success. The board needs to understand that the chief executive can be effective only if the board is supportive and respectful.

Chief executives have serious responsibilities with regard to their accountability to boards. They have to establish and achieve organizational goals and to develop a "weather report" or a "dashboard" that shows the board, on a quarterly basis, just how well the organization is doing or not doing, in accordance with organizational plans. As soon as plans are not yielding results, chief executives must discuss the situation with their boards and lay out the challenges, remedies, and alternative plans. Good chief executives draw on the business acumen of board members to help shape the issues and devise and adapt organizational plans. The board should support the chief executive in leading the organization, but the chief executive is obliged to keep the board informed about programmatic results—the attainment of mission—and about financial indicators.

For example, if one of a public university's primary strategic interests is expanding enrollments in order to enhance support, and the chief executive has developed a plan to make that happen, then the chief executive must provide a quarterly or semi-annual accounting to the board, including a concise analysis of the reasons for success or failure, remedies if necessary, and continuing courses of action. Part of the chief executive's job is to put the programmatic and financial results in the context of various environmental forces, such as state budget cuts or the decline or resurgence of the commercial health of the region.

Boards should conduct an annual assessment of their chief executives. In order for the review to accelerate the organization's progress rather than create tension and duress, the review process should be conducted thoughtfully and fairly. The process should be led by the board chair, who should be most familiar with the chief executive through their partnership relationship; in some situations, though, another leading board member may be better suited to conduct the review—someone who has a particular rapport with the chief executive or human resource expertise. Larger organizations often form a special board committee to evaluate the chief executive and the compensation package; smaller nonprofits may simply designate key board officers to perform this role.

Board members can be asked to submit comments on the executive's ability to lead, supply a vision, fundraise, collaborate with the board, communicate with key constituents about the value of the organization, build and lead the staff, and assume other key leadership responsibilities, as outlined in Exhibit 5.1. The input of members of the executive committee—board officers and committee chairs—can be particularly helpful because they are most familiar with the executive's effectiveness and style. However, the board member leading the assessment must filter the input of board members to make sure that it is valid and thoughtful. Comments from board members who are not engaged or as knowledgeable as they believe they are or who have personal agendas should be discounted if not discarded. A board chair who has a personal agenda that interferes with making good judgments can be a detriment in the evaluation of the chief executive; in this case, fellow board officers—vice chairs, the board secretary, the board treasurer—share the authority and responsibility to ensure that the evaluation is fair and constructive.

In assessing the chief executive, it is not appropriate for the board to solicit staff input. The chief executive is fully responsible

Exhibit 5.1. Assessing the CEO.

To assess the CEO, the board chair should ask board members to evaluate the extent to which the CEO:

Articulates a compelling mission and vision based on opportunities to add value in the community

Defines a strategic direction with a clear path to achieve success, including a viable revenue model

Provides clear and concise information to the board, on a quarterly basis, regarding the organization's relationships with key funders, programmatic outcomes, financial status, new opportunities and ways to achieve success, new challenges and ways to address them

Is a compelling spokesperson for the organization and its mission

Works effectively with board members, making clear how they can be helpful and then recognizing their contributions

Builds and leads a capable staff team

---

for building a capable staff, earning their respect and loyalty, and mentoring and guiding them. Because good leadership is essential to organizational effectiveness, organizational outcomes are evidence of the chief executive's success or failure. Additionally, attentive board members, especially officers and committee chairs, have fairly clear impressions of how the chief executive leads the staff and how respected he or she is. Soliciting staff input in order to evaluate the chief executive is also destructive to the institution. When board members cross the line by interacting with the staff in this way, they undermine the chief executive's relationship with the staff. If a board needs to solicit staff input in order to evaluate the chief executive, it does not have sufficient measures and reports of organizational outcomes or does not understand the work of the organization.

In conducting the review, the board should keep in mind that the chief executive's effectiveness depends on the board's effectiveness, so the board should look at itself as well. If the organization has failed to accomplish certain goals, the board needs to consider how it can actively collaborate with the chief executive. For example, when an organization seeks to strengthen its funding streams, the board as well as the chief executive needs to be engaged. The board certainly has a role in fundraising; additionally, in some cases, board members can help the institution financially by lobbying legislators for public funding or for revision of the rules that are restricting the organization's effectiveness. If pending legislation will force nonprofit organizations to conduct costly audits, above and beyond what seems necessary, or to vet volunteers to such an extent that the cost is prohibitive, then board members can be valuable in educating legislators. The chief executive cannot maximize any organization's results without quality board support.

Serious matters regarding the chief executive's performance should never wait until the annual review. Weaknesses need to be dealt with as they occur. In some cases, the board can strengthen the executive by providing resources for training, consulting, or coaching. If the board has concerns about the satisfaction of key funders with regard to organizational reporting and outcomes, then board members should meet with key funders; this way, board members can be aware of any failings on the part of the organization and ensure that the issues are remedied. If the board determines that the executive does not have the ability to lead the organization effectively, the board should document the issues and prepare for a separation. Boards cannot afford to shy away from firing an executive who is not performing. As one board member noted, "Love 'em, or fire 'em."

Nonprofit boards need to recognize the importance to their executives of thoughtful and constructive support and guidance, including positive feedback when it is earned. Richard Moyers, program officer at the Agnes and Eugene Meyer Foundation, in Washington, D.C., notes that "nonprofit executives usually work under a fair amount of duress. They are passionate about their organizations, and they dedicate enormous energies to their jobs. It is too often disheartening for nonprofit executives when board members fail to appreciate the value of the executive's contribution and effectiveness" (interview, January 7, 2004).

The assessment of the chief executive is indeed personal, and the dynamics can be highly charged. Whoever leads the assessment needs to ensure that the process is useful, positive, and productive in helping the chief executive to continue leading the organization or in raising his or her effectiveness. The board leader or leaders who meet with the chief executive to conduct the evaluation should be sure to fully recognize achievements; be clear about areas of performance that need to be addressed; and clearly articulate expectations. In the course of the evaluation discussion, the board should ask the chief executive how the board can be helpful and supportive in addressing key challenges and opportunities.

Setting the Mission, Vision, and Strategic Direction

In today's highly complex and sophisticated nonprofit environment, the chief executive must take the lead in shaping the mission and vision and establishing the strategic direction for the organization. Boards usually comprise people who are amateurs with regard to the organization's mission, which may be in areas they are not familiar with. Furthermore, board members are involved with the nonprofit organization on a limited, part-time basis, rarely enough time to fully grasp the revenue model or the best practices in the field.

An effective chief executive knows that the way to leverage board-member expertise and enthusiasm and engage the board's support is to elevate the board's knowledge of the sector, focus the board on the major organizational opportunities, and solicit board-member input in shaping the mission, vision, and strategic direction. The way to energize and inspire the board is to involve them in meaty discussions of organizational purpose and direction. After having these discussions a good CEO incorporates board input in developing the mission, vision, and key strategic directions, presents these statements to the board for further discussion, and then finalizes the plan with the additional board-member comments. If board members are in conflict regarding their vision of the future, outside consultants can be helpful as facilitators. In most cases, however, if the chief executive prepares good information for the board, board members will be able to come to a consensus on future directions. James Quigley, CEO of Deloitte & Touche USA LLP, comments that "there is a clear distinction between high functioning and low functioning nonprofits. The most effective nonprofits are governed by boards that state and restate the organization's mission, vision, and strategic direction. When board members understand what the organization seeks to accomplish, they can provide valuable assistance to drive towards success. Boards should have thoughtful, probing discussions of key strategic issues. When board members are called on to provide intellectual capital, they will become more deeply engaged and more fully committed than if they are only asked to write checks" (interview, June 8, 2004).

Thus, the board's role is to come to consensus on the organization's focus and direction, ensure that the chief executive has a plan that is in accordance with the overall purpose, and hold the chief executive accountable for achieving organizational purposes in serving the community. Consequently, when setting the strategic direction for the organization, the chief executive needs to determine how the organization will measure success in both qualitative and quantitative terms. Ultimately, the board must be able to assess the extent to which the organization is achieving its mission, the effectiveness of its services, the costs of providing services, and the revenue model. In some cases, organizational success can be measured and reported without great expense or complication. For example, a job-training service can determine how many people were trained, how many were hired after training, the cost for each person trained and placed, how much the clients earned in salaries once they were placed, how many received health care benefits, and how long they stayed employed. The chief executive, with help from staff, should also show comparable figures for organizations that provide such services in other cities. With this information, board members can make a judgment regarding the organization's effectiveness and whether the chief executive needs to make changes in order to achieve greater efficiencies or results; understand the value and utility of the organization; and make the case for the merits of the organization and its services. In some cases, measurement is elusive and costly, especially when longitudinal studies are called for and many factors may influence outcomes.

In spite of the challenges, the chief executive must find ways to assess and communicate the value and relevance of the organization's programs and services especially as they relate to achieving the mission. Boards should expect this information, become familiar with it, and use it to make strategic decisions about the future. For example, if an organization that reaches out to homeless men with mental illnesses can show through its numbers that it is succeeding in connecting men to treatment centers, but the organization is not able to fund itself as a free-standing organization, then the board should seek to save the outreach programs by folding them into a larger social service center. In order to make this decision, the board needs to see solid information about how many men have been successfully served, the cost per man served, comparisons with similar programs elsewhere, the interest of funders in continuing to support the services, and the viability of moving the services to a larger organization. The executive director, who should be an expert in this field and who should have the financial information, should lay this information out for the board; if the executive director is not capable of doing so, then board members need to step in.

Most important of all, the board's role is to engage in discussions with the chief executive to imagine the future and bring it about. For example, one organization's most vital program was to collect surplus food from restaurants and food markets and then deliver the food to shelters that serve homeless people. When the organization found itself struggling financially, the board pursued a merger with a larger nonprofit organization in order to sustain the services. These are circumstances when the chief executive needs to provide the board with data for decision making (such as number of people fed and the cost of providing each pound of food to each person). Given relevant information, the board can work with the chief executive to imagine and achieve a vision of the future for the betterment of the community.

Board members cannot be passive bystanders in this process. For example, in response to a dramatic presentation by the chief executive of a future course of action for an organization, one board officer commented to the CEO, "We will see," meaning we will see how you do with this project and whether it works. This is not the proper approach. The board's role is to hear the case for a new direction or opportunity, determine whether it is worthy given the organization's mission, and then ask how the board can help achieve success. Not "We will see" but "We will help make this happen."

Developing Support for the Organization

The board has a vital role in ensuring that the organization has the resources it needs to achieve its mission. To begin with, all board members should make financial contributions to the organization to the best of their ability. Although board-member contributions may not represent a significant portion of the organization's revenues, board members must demonstrate their commitment to the organization through unanimous participation in giving. Surprisingly, this basic board expectation is not fulfilled in all organizations.

Additionally, all board members should be part of an effort coordinated by the board chair and chief executive to generate resources. The organization can provide programs and services only to the extent that it has the financial means to do so. According to Fisher Howe, an expert on nonprofit governance and fundraising, "Responsibility for attracting resources lies with the board. It cannot pass on to anyone else the responsibility for the resources to sustain the programs—not to the staff, not to a committee, not to an outside consultant or agent" (Howe, 1995, p. 51).

Board members should be recruited and engaged for the specific purpose of helping to ensure organizational viability by providing expertise, funding, and community support. Some board members have access to corporate dollars or wealthy individuals. Others can participate with senior staff in meetings with key funders in order to make the case on behalf of the organization. Yet others can organize "friend-raising" events to expose their friends and acquaintances to the compelling work of the organization or can simply host their friends at the organization's events. Board members with expertise in advocacy, public relations, or sales can help the organization frame its case and present it to the right audiences. For example, a young executive from Enterprise Rent-a-Car was able to make a useful contribution as soon as he joined a nonprofit by helping it package corporate sponsorship levels for an upcoming fundraising event; he knew from his sales experience what would work. This project yielded significant new revenues for the organization.

An organization's success in fundraising depends on its having a board that comprises individuals with a broad variety of backgrounds and from diverse communities. A board that is homogeneous will be able to look for support in only one narrow segment of the community. For example, a cultural institution that establishes relationships with homes for senior adults, group homes for those who are disabled, African Americans, Asian Americans, Latinos, schools that have diverse student bodies, and religious groups can expand its opportunities to serve as well as maximize funding potential from foundations, individuals, and public sources. Board members with a variety of backgrounds understand these opportunities best and can encourage and support broad community relationships and make valuable introductions.

In today's tough fiscal environment, almost every nonprofit needs to revisit its revenue model and update it to address new challenges as well as new opportunities. Board members who are organizational strategists with business skills can be particularly helpful to the chief executive and the board in explaining the financial issues, implications, and options. Ultimately, the board's role is to consider the plans that are presented for discussion and to make the final decisions. In addition, all board members should help in making introductions to prospective donors or partners, making and asking for contributions, and representing the organization in meetings with funders when asked. The key is for the board to take ownership of the funding strategy as a factor of great consequence for organizational success.

Ensuring Organizational Integrity

The board is the guardian of the mission and the tax-exempt status of the organization. The board and chief executive must be diligent in recognizing the organization's charitable mission as its guiding light in all decision making. As Quigley explains, "Whereas for-profit boards are stewards of shareholder dollars, nonprofit boards are stewards of the public's money. Boards are accountable for the organization's dollars and how they are used. With effective board oversight, the public can have confidence that their funds are being used well to serve the community's interests" (interview, June 8, 2004). The mission statement should appear on all board agendas and promotional materials as a constant reminder of the organization's purpose, and the board must constantly consider its responsibility to the community.

In order to fulfill its responsibility for financial oversight, the board should receive complete, accurate, understandable, and timely financial reports (such as Worksheet 5.1), at least quarterly, from the chief executive. The board should also have a treasurer who is a volunteer board member, not a paid staff member, and a finance committee that reviews and monitors the annual budget. An auditor works with the chief executive and staff to conduct the audit, but a separate board audit committee should select, hire, and meet directly with the auditor, with or without the chief executive and staff present. This private meeting provides an opportunity for candor and for ensuring board confidence in the financial reports and internal systems. Finally, the board should establish sound investment policies and a separate investment committee if there are sufficient funds to oversee.

As advocates for the organization, board members must be certain that the organization lives up to the community's expectations for effectiveness, integrity, and accountability. Having a well-qualified board treasurer and audit committee can provide the board with the information that it needs to know about the organization's fiduciary integrity. Having programmatic information from the chief executive can give the board confidence, if merited, in the organization's effectiveness and relevance.

Setting the Big Agenda

The board chair and chief executive should set aside a board meeting at least once a year specifically to discuss and articulate the key strategic challenges and opportunities facing the organization—in other words, to determine exactly how the board can advance the organization as it looks to the future. The board chair or the chief executive can facilitate the meeting or can designate a board member or outside facilitator to do so. In any case, the chief executive should be regarded as the leading expert regarding the work of the organization, and the chief executive should prepare and provide the board with clear, concise, and accurate information that will be useful in understanding the key issues, the decisions to be made, and the implications of particular choices and decisions. Every board member should be encouraged to attend and participate in this important discussion. Key points should be noted on an easel. Ultimately, the board should decide on two to five key strategic issues. For most nonprofit organizations, the issues of consequence are related to relevance, effectiveness, communications, and financial structure.

Worksheet 5.1. Assessing the Financial Situation.

1. **Total organizational budget:** _____

2. **Revenue**

Revenue Sources for Annual Operating Fund	Percent of Operating Budget	Prospects for This Revenue Source	Possible Remedies If Needed
Foundation grants			
Fees for services			
Federal funds			
State funds			
County funds			
Endowment income			
Personal contributions			
Fundraising events			
Other (please specify) _____			

3. **Based on the key revenue sources and potential opportunities or vulnerabilities, which financial issues require the board's and CEO's primary focus and attention?** _____

4. **How much is the operating cash reserve?**   In dollars: _____   In months of operating funds: _____

5. **If the answer to #4 is "less than four months of operating expenses in the cash reserve," then**

   Is this shortfall related to the timing of revenue? ☐ yes ☐ no

   Does the board receive a monthly cash-flow statement in order to be alert to a cash crunch? ☐ yes   ☐ no

   What is the board's plan in case of a lack of sufficient operating cash? _____

The board should focus in particular on the financial model: the overall commitment of resources that is needed to provide high-impact, mission-oriented services, as well as the revenue structure. In considering how to generate resources, the board needs to consider each significant funding source with regard to its potential. In order to ensure the nonprofit's financial sustainability, the board and the chief executive need to develop a formula for a combination of revenue sources. The board should look to the chief executive to provide essential information about opportunities for revenue enhancement, costs of key programs, potential funding losses, and alternative revenue models. The board should also expect the chief executive to develop and provide measures of organizational success and impact and to develop the case for support. As a strategic matter, the board needs to communicate the importance of the organization to key constituents and needs to determine who values the organization and how it will gain future support. The chief executive may call on individual board members to leverage their business expertise, insight, and perspectives, and would be wise to incorporate board members' input. By drawing on board members for support and input, the chief executive can formulate the case for the organization, its financial model, and outcome measurements.

Most important, the organization needs to candidly assess its relevance to the community. Often organizations need to update themselves about priority issues. Education and economic development are often among the public's top concerns. The chief executive should be knowledgeable about public interests in order to gauge opportunities for support. The chief executive can gain valuable insight from board members who have key relationships in the community and can engage the board in discussions of community priorities and the implications for the organization and its future.

Imagining the future and helping to achieve it is the most fundamental role of the board. The board needs to be engaged in bringing about progress toward the accomplishment of the mission and the vision. Boards are most effective when they focus on the issues that matter most.

Establishing Expectations and Accountability for Board Members

In order to advance the mission of the organization and meet fiduciary responsibilities, board members must be committed to the organizations they serve. Legal responsibilities include the duties of care, loyalty, and obedience discussed previously in this chapter. In order to make these responsibilities clear, the board should establish a statement of expectations of every board member: meeting attendance, contributions, fundraising, committee participation, and any other relevant duties. Exhibit 5.2 is an example of such a statement. The statement of expectations is helpful for current board members as well as for prospective new members. By understanding exactly what is required, they can avoid being surprised or disappointed. Once the board has agreed on board-member expectations, uninvolved board members can step off graciously. In many cases, board members are relieved to disengage; they simply need the opportunity.

Creating a statement of expectations is fairly straightforward. The statement is meaningless, however, unless the board also establishes a system of accountability. The board governance committee, a contemporary version of the traditional board nominating committee, should ensure that all board members either are participating productively or are removed. The staff should track board-member attendance, giving, and involvement for the board governance committee.

When large donors expect it, the board can create honorary positions without governance responsibility. Major contributors deserve recognition and they should hold seats of honor, but such roles of distinction need not involve the responsibilities that go with board service.

Exhibit 5.2. Sample Statement of Expectations for Board Members.

Role and Responsibilities

The following responsibilities are specific to (Organization Name) and are articulated for the purpose of complementing or clarifying certain aspects of the traditional governing responsibilities of board members.

1. **Commit to the mission and goals of (Organization Name).**

2. **Attend meetings of the Board of Directors:** *(Four)* meetings are scheduled each year. Board members are encouraged to attend all *(four)* meetings (they are scheduled more than one year in advance). Minimum attendance expected of each individual Board member is *(75 percent)*.

3. **Serve on at least one committee and attend committee meetings:** Board members are encouraged to attend all meetings of the committees on which they serve. However, attendance at *(50 percent)* of the meetings is expected at a minimum.

4. **Contribute expertise and participate in the strategic development of the Board and *(Organization Name)*.**

5. **Attend *(Organization Name)* special events.**

6. **Make a personal contribution to *(Organization Name)*:** Every member of the Board of Directors is expected to make a financial contribution in addition to in-kind contributions of time and resources.

7. **Develop funding support:** Assist the *(Organization Name)* Board and staff in membership-development and fundraising efforts by arranging introductions, signing letters to friends and associates, and otherwise opening doors to funding sources. Each Board member who represents a corporation is asked to seek organizational support at the highest possible level of sponsorship.

8. **Represent *(Organization Name)*:** Be familiar with and speak in support of *(Organization Name)* and allow his/her name to be used in support of *(Organization Name)*'s mission.

9. **Disclose any potential conflict of interest with *(Organization Name)*.**

I understand that as a member of the Board of Directors of (Organization Name), I will be held accountable for meeting the expectations above on an annual basis.

_____   _____

Signature   *Date*

Resolving Governance Problems: Red Flags

Board members need to remain alert to the possibility that an organization's governance structure needs improvement. It can be difficult for a board member or chief executive to determine whether a board or organization needs help. To make it simpler, using this list of symptoms to ascertain how well a board is functioning can make board members aware of when it is time to explore remedies, probably with an outside facilitator. A board experiencing three or more of the items below is in distress. These problems, some of which are discussed in more detail in Chapter Six, can indeed be addressed, but they require attention or the organization will suffer, as will all who are involved.

1. The average attendance rate at board meetings is 60 percent or lower.

2. At meetings the board discusses small matters and does not address large organizational issues.

3. The chief executive's performance review includes anonymous and critical comments around which there is no clear consensus.

4. The board chair has substantial personal resources but is not a leading donor to the organization.

5. The board chair is not encouraging board members to contribute to the organization.

6. More than a third of the board members have been on the board for at least six years.

7. Board discussions are dominated by three or four individuals.

8. Board members who have been on the board for fewer than two years rarely participate in discussions at meetings.

9. Board meetings consist of reports rather than discussion.

10. Board meetings go on beyond the scheduled time for adjournment.

11. Materials are not sent to the board in advance of meetings (or the materials are lengthy and difficult to understand).

12. The chief executive is expressing his frustrations to board members in conversations on the side.

13. Board members are not aware of the size of the organization's budget, the key funding sources, or the overall financial situation.

14. The board is not clear about the mission of the organization or its vision.

Exhibit 5.3 lists some common governance problems boards may face and suggests remedies that board members can implement to improve outcomes.

The Bottom Line

Governance needs to be taken seriously. Nonprofits perform vital work in service to the community, and boards should not treat their role lightly. Boards that take the time to understand what it means to govern and that determine how they can improve and strengthen their organizations serve the community well and help the nonprofit sector achieve its fullest potential.

In order to advance their organizations, boards thus need to be clear about their roles and responsibilities, to determine the big agenda, to be accountable themselves, to assess and improve when necessary the way they govern, and to commit themselves to their organizations' success in serving the community.

Exhibit 5.3. Governance Troubleshooting Checklist.

Symptoms	Possible Diagnosis	Remedies	Outcomes
Average attendance at board meetings is less than 60 percent.	The board is too large	Downsize the board so that each person's participation matters	Attendance is more consistent; board members are more fully engaged and knowledgeable
	Expectations for attendance are not clear	Create a statement of expectations	
	Meetings wander and address minor matters	Focus meeting agendas on strategic issues	The board addresses key strategic issues
	Meetings are held at an inconvenient time and/or location	Survey the board to find the best time and place	The board comprises members who are committed
	Meetings are not scheduled far enough in advance	Schedule meetings far enough in advance and stick to the schedule	
	Meetings are too frequent	Reduce frequency; create committees as needed	

Exhibit 5.3. Governance Troubleshooting Checklist, *continued*.

Symptoms	Possible Diagnosis	Remedies	Outcomes
Board meetings focus on minor matters rather than on strategic issues.	Board meetings are too frequent	Reduce frequency	The board is productive
	The board needs to understand the strategic issues	Devote meetings to a few key issues; educate the board about the factors that affect the future of the organization and key opportunities	
	The chair needs to focus meeting discussions	Have the CEO assist the chair in understanding the key issues; provide mentoring, coaching, consulting to the chair; or plan chair succession	
All board members are not making financial contributions and participating in fundraising.	Expectations of the board are not clear	Create a statement of expectations and hold members accountable	The community and funders see a committed board and feel encouraged to support the organization
	The board chair is not leading by example or urging board support	Provide coaching or mentoring to the board chair; or plan chair succession	
	Board members do not understand how their financial support can improve the community	Have the CEO and chair educate the board	The organization has funds (from the board) to do good work

Symptom	Possible Cause	Action	Desired Outcome
The CEO is expressing dissatisfaction.	The CEO is not adequately supported by board	Have the board, led by the chair, demonstrate support through actions, words, and suitable compensation	The organization achieves results under capable and satisfied leadership
	The CEO is not capable of doing the job	Provide the CEO with coaching or training; or remove the CEO if necessary	
The organization lacks a clear vision or plan.	The CEO is not qualified to lead the board and organization in creating a vision and plan	Provide training, coaching, consulting to the CEO; or replace the CEO	The organization achieves useful outcomes for the community
	Board members do not have the relevant skills, talents, diversity, relationships to assist the CEO	Rebuild the board	
A financial deficit is looming.	The CEO is not qualified to diagnose and remedy financial problems	Provide training, coaching, consulting to the CEO; or replace the CEO	The organization has the resources to achieve useful outcomes for the community
	Board members do not have the relevant skills, talents, diversity, relationships to assist the CEO	Rebuild the board	
	The organization is not sustainable with its current structure	Have the CEO and board explore new models, possibly with a consultant	

6

Building Better Boards

Providing a Sound Structure

To love a place you must participate in the
community and give back something in return
for all you receive.
　　　　　　—*Isabel Allende*, My Invented Country, 2003

How can a board organize itself in a logical way to address its big agenda? A board structure is a format for allocating the precious resource of time to maximize efficiency and effectiveness. The task of structuring a board flows logically once the board is clear about its role, understands the key issues for its attention, and has set expectations for members.

To illustrate, imagine two extremes (which, unfortunately, are not unheard of). At one end of the spectrum, consider a board that meets once or twice a year and has fifty members. Such a board is unlikely to fulfill its fiduciary responsibilities of oversight or play a relevant role in maintaining the organization's effectiveness and viability. At the other extreme, imagine a board that meets fifteen times a year, for three hours per meeting, late into the evening, and spends time examining accounts receivable and hearing staff reports. This board is also not likely to be leading the organization to maximize its revenues and adapt its programs and services for high impact in the community. This board probably could not even recruit or retain people with vision, creativity, and strategic expertise.

Realigning Board Structure

Given that the boards described above are not good models, what is the best structure for a board? The matters to consider are size, frequency and duration of board meetings, and committees and their roles.

Board Size

How many members does it take to perform the work of a board? Optimal board size varies from one organization to another. An organization that depends on broad and diverse constituencies for grants, contributions, and fees for services may need a large board with members who have reach into many corners of the community. An organization that relies primarily on third-party payers, such as insurance companies, state Medicaid funds, and federal Medicare, may need a small board that provides oversight of major financial and strategic matters.

In any case, a well-functioning board is unlikely to comprise more than twenty-five individuals. When people are part of larger groups, they lose a sense of personal responsibility; larger boards cannot actively engage all members. However, most nonprofits need at least ten board members in order to have access to the community as well as to certain kinds of expertise. Therefore, somewhere between ten and twenty-five is probably a good size for most boards.

Frequency of Meetings

Most boards find that meeting four times per year for ninety minutes is optimal. Each board meeting should focus on key strategic issues and not on information sharing, announcements, and lesser matters that can be handled through other sorts of communications. The chief executive should make sure that the board receives timely, accurate, relevant, and concise information prior to each board meeting. The chief executive should help prepare the board chair and committee chairs to focus on key issues at the board meeting and should anticipate the time that will be needed for the most important matters and schedule them at the top of the meeting.

Board members are contributing precious time to advance the mission of the organization. Nonprofits are sure to lose their most valuable board members if meeting time is wasted on trivia, materials are not sent out in advance, and materials are not clear and useful. By keeping their boards focused, and using the time well, chief executives can help their organizations attract and retain high-caliber board members whose time is in great demand.

Committees

Committees, not the board as a whole, should delve deeply into key issues and work with the chief executive to develop and present coherent recommendations to the board. Board meetings should be used to focus the full board's attention on high-impact organizational issues that have been studied by board committees in concert with the chief executive and expert staff members or consultants. For example, the board's investments committee might work with the chief executive, or his chief financial officer, to study the organization's investment policies to ensure that they maximize returns while also being reasonably stable and secure. The board treasurer or the committee chair should then report the recommendations of the committee to the board and address questions. The board chair should ask for a board vote to approve the committee's recommendations. If board members have pressing questions that are not satisfactorily answered by the committee, the board chair might ask the committee to review the issues and call for a vote at a subsequent board meeting.

The chair plays the key role in deciding when to advance a discussion to a vote and when to ask for further information and follow-up from the chief executive or further study by a committee. A skilled board chair listens carefully and asks a few board members for their comments, perhaps calling on people whose experience and judgment the chair respects. The chair not only considers the validity of the concern that is raised but also the level of traction it is receiving with various board members. The board should respect the recommendations of a committee that has expertise and that has devoted study to an issue such as the investments policy; the board chair should not stop progress every time a board member raises a concern. However, the board chair should not push for a vote if board members find legitimate problems with a committee's recommendations. This situation underscores the vital role of the board chair, which is addressed further in the next chapter. The chair needs constantly to balance board-member concerns and the pace of decision making so that legitimate issues are addressed, while progress is not unreasonably delayed.

Each board needs to create a committee structure that makes sense. The chief executive is an important partner to the board in determining the optimal structure. The chief executive can make sure the committees are aligned with key strategic issues, that staff members are assigned and are prepared to produce the information that each committee needs, and also that the board structure makes sense given organizational resources such as staff and board-member time. For example, boards and committees that meet more often than necessary tax the staff and the organization and scare away board members who seek a governing role, not an operational or management role, in the organization. Boards and committees that meet too often invariably begin to deal with administrative rather than board matters.

In most cases, the board needs a finance committee to ensure that the organization has a sound budget and to provide oversight; an audit committee to select and work with the auditor; a development committee to finalize an aggressive but realistic fundraising plan that can be supported by all board members; an investments committee to ensure that the most reliable and profitable investment policies and approaches are in place; and a governance committee to work with the chief executive to identify and engage board members, select the organization's officers, and ensure that board members are involved according to the statement of expectations. Optional committees that might also be useful for particular organizations include quality oversight, facilities planning, strategic alliances, and community relations.

Board committees that comprise carefully selected board members can address key issues in depth. For example, a community-relations committee made up of members who have important relationships in diverse communities can assist the chief executive and the staff in outreach and in arranging meetings with key stakeholders or potential partners. Committee members might also involve other board members or even non-board members in outreach and education.

Boards should exercise caution in establishing committees that might interfere with staff functions. For example, human resources and marketing planning are areas of staff work for an organization with an experienced and sophisticated management team. Appropriately qualified nonprofit chief executives and their executive teams have the expertise to develop strategic plans, and they will implement organizational plans for finance, marketing, development, human resources, community relations, and other key management areas. Nevertheless, effective chief executives often access volunteer management assistance on an ad hoc basis from board members with useful expertise or relationships. For large projects, the executive staff may even hire outside experts.

Boards should establish ad hoc committees when specific and timely issues need study and review at the board level. Ad hoc committees can work for as long as necessary and then dissolve when their work is done. They should not be allowed to develop a life of their own and become difficult to dismantle when their function becomes obsolete. A committee that lives beyond its usefulness can become a burden to the board, the staff, and the organization. For example, an ad hoc committee might be set up to review possible new organizational alliances. Although the chief executive and the board chair are the key leaders in initial discussions with potential partners, at some point a board committee might be helpful to the chief executive in studying the financial and programmatic implications of an alliance as well as the new organizational and governance structure that would be needed.

Committees are effective only when they have well-qualified committee chairs, a staff member who is assigned by the chief executive to support the committee (perhaps the chief executive herself or himself), and a small group of committee members who have relevant experience and expertise and who are committed to the work of the committee. A well-run committee requires excellent staff support to set up meetings, prepare and distribute useful and concise information, take notes, and follow up. Worksheet 6.1 is a grid boards can use to realign their committee structure.

Executive Committee

Although the full board should participate in organizational governance, creating an executive committee comprising board officers and committee chairs can be useful. Executive committee meetings provide the opportunity for the chief executive and board chair to have substantive discussions about key organizational issues and strategies and to coordinate committee activities. As an example, consider an organization that provides shelter and support for

Worksheet 6.1. Proposed Committee Structure.

Current Structure	Proposed Structure			
Current Committees	Proposed Committees	Frequency of Meetings	Board Members	Members from Professional Staff

women and children who are victims of domestic violence. If 70 percent of this organization's funding is from the state, and state funding is set to be cut in the coming year, then this matter needs to be raised at an executive committee meeting by the finance chair (who is also the board treasurer in most cases), the board chair, the chief executive, and the development chair (who is charged with fundraising). In addition, the discussion needs to include the governance (nominating) chair because of implications for the recruitment of new board members with regard to their fundraising potential and ability to give. If the board traditionally, for example, comprises mostly women who are grassroots supporters, the drop in state funding may prompt the board to consider recruiting businesspeople or opening the board to men as well as women who are interested in the mission and in helping to develop new revenue streams.

To give a real-life example, as the result of a discussion in the executive committee at a domestic-violence center about devising a new strategy for recruiting young businesspeople, both men and women, for board positions, a matchmaker recommended the first male candidate to the board. The new board member, an investment broker around thirty years old, had the idea of holding a fundraising luncheon with a national speaker. The luncheon has since become a successful annual event that attracts over one thousand people (including many who come with corporate sponsorship) and features speakers like Gloria Steinem, Denise Brown (sister of Nicole Simpson), and Jean Harris (convicted of killing Dr. Herman Tarnower). The luncheons net over $70,000 a year, almost 8 percent of the organization's annual operating budget.

A chief executive who is empowered to lead is the single most valuable asset to the executive committee in identifying the key issues for board attention, working with the board chair to create substantive and well-focused committee discussions, providing useful planning information, coordinating follow-up with board committees and the staff, and making sure that matters of importance are also discussed at board meetings. To the extent that the CEO can educate the executive committee about the most significant organizational matters, the executive committee can become an asset in advancing the organization. Because it takes time and effort for board members, who are usually not experts in the field of service, to understand the strategic challenges, the executive committee provides an important forum and opportunity for the board leadership to elevate its understanding and rally the full board to engage effectively in supporting the nonprofit and its mission.

In most cases, the executive committee should meet once before each board meeting. This schedule allows a continuous flow of board involvement in organizational issues and decisions of consequence. It also provides time for the proper preparation of board agendas and of materials that can be sent to the board in advance of meetings.

Governance Committee

A strong and capable governance committee is essential for board effectiveness. This committee has a year-round responsibility to develop the board. In the past, boards had nominating committees. Unfortunately, nominating committees often met once a year for a last-minute conversation about people to bring on to the board. Worse, nominating-committee members often considered candidates only from among their narrow circles of friends, business colleagues, or golfing associates, and their review of candidate qualifications was perfunctory at best. Today's governance committee has a far more substantial role in identifying the skills, expertise, diversity, and relationships that are needed on the board in order to advance the organization. The committee has to consider the kinds of people the board needs, identify and assess potential candidates, meet with candidates to establish their level of commitment and interest, and present the candidates' qualifications to the board.

The chief executive is a key asset to the governance committee in anticipating the areas of expertise and relationships that will be most useful. For example, the chief executive can identify segments of the community that have not been included on the board, conduct outreach, and suggest candidates who have shown interest in and support for the nonprofit. An organization whose board comprises only wealthy suburbanites or corporate leaders may need to reach out to successful, young entrepreneurs who are African American, Latino, Asian American, or from urban areas so that the board addresses broad community concerns and new opportunities for support and participation.

Additionally, the governance committee ensures that the organization has a statement of expectations of board members, that board members are performing according to the expectations, and that new board members are fully aware of their responsibilities and prepared to fulfill their them. Business Volunteers Unlimited's experience in engaging over one thousand board candidates on almost three hundred nonprofit boards shows that candidates appreciate knowing what will be expected of them. Candidates also respect an organization that has given some thought to the role of the new board member and has the courtesy to explain its expectations up front.

The governance committee also considers the educational needs of the board. For example, funding and service-delivery models for health care are highly complex. Members of a health care organization's board need educational sessions and good written materials in order to be prepared to make governance decisions. Although a capable chief executive should arrange for board members to have the materials they need, the governance committee can be helpful to the chief executive in exploring ways to deepen the board's knowledge. For example, the board of a small, local arts-education organization can benefit from learning about national best practices in order to envision new possibilities for programming. The chief executive or outside guest speakers can be helpful in providing this broad perspective.

The governance committee should also decide when to conduct a board assessment with an expert facilitator. Because the board's role is so essential to organizational success, and it is all too easy to fall into old habits, having an outsider lead a board discussion about governance can illuminate opportunities to strengthen the board. An expert facilitator begins the process by meeting with the board chair and chief executive for their input, then surveys all board members and interviews many of them in person or by phone, and finally compiles a summary report of the board's assessment of itself. The report helps the board understand members' expectations and how they perceive their role, the extent to which members are aware of key financial and strategic issues, and the ability of current board practices to engage board members in productive work. The board assessment should culminate in a board retreat where the facilitator leads the board in making changes to its practices in order to be clear about expectations of board members and to adjust the board structure (size and frequency of meetings), committee structure (kinds of committees, their charges, and their composition), and board composition. Worksheets 6.2 and 6.3 are examples of forms that boards can use to assess themselves, refocus on more current strategic issues, update board composition, and establish clear board member expectations.

Boards should conduct an annual or bi-annual assessment because boards and organizations are constantly evolving as community issues and needs change, old funding streams dry up, and new opportunities emerge. The right board composition and structure in the past is unlikely to be the right composition and structure today and tomorrow. To be effective, boards need to continuously develop and update themselves. To take a glaring example, consider the composition of the board of an art museum or symphony orchestra in the 1950s and then look at the board composition of the same organization today. The contrast is striking and obvious. The board no longer comprises only white Protestants of enormous wealth but a mix of people of different religions and races, small-business owners and educators, as well as corporate leaders. Boards have become more inclusive so that organizations can reach broader audiences as

Worksheet 6.2. Strengthening Governance.

Key institutional issues: What are the *threats* that challenge your organization—that will "make or break" your organization in the next three to five years? What are the *opportunities* for the organization to more effectively serve the community?

Board Involvement/Effectiveness	Where Are You?	Where Do You Want to Be?	How Will You Get There?
1. Board focuses its attention and energy on key institutional and strategic issues. • Agendas of board meetings are focused on key institutional/strategic issues. • Committees are created/structured around key institutional issues, not simply organizational functions.			
2. Board gives and raises money. • All board members make a contribution. • Board members understand various ways they can help to raise money. • All board members actively help to raise money.			
3. Every board member has particular skills, expertise, or community relationships that are useful to the organization in dealing with key strategic issues. The board includes members with all the skills, expertise, and community relationships that are needed.			

Worksheet 6.2. **Strengthening Governance,** *continued.*

Board Involvement/Effectiveness	Where Are You?	Where Do You Want to Be?	How Will You Get There?
4. The board has confidence in the CEO's ability to lead and manage; conducts an annual performance review to encourage and support the CEO; and empowers the CEO to manage the organization.			
5. The board reviews the organization's finances at least four times per year; all board members understand the financial reports; an annual audit is conducted by an outside auditor for the board.			
6. The board has set into place a mechanism (committee) to evaluate its composition and effectiveness on an annual basis.			

Worksheet 6.3. Board Self-Assessment.

Conduct a board session to address the following:

1. Can the board identify the key strategic opportunities and challenges facing the organization?

What are they?

2. How can the board and board members help the CEO advance the organization to achieve its mission? (e.g., attend meetings; make personal financial contributions; make introductions to valuable supporters; advocate for the organization with key constituents; provide expertise)

What are board members doing to fulfill their roles?

3. How can the board be supportive of the CEO? (e.g., provide an appropriate compensation package; provide positive feedback when it is deserved; provide access to training, coaching, and consulting services)

What is the board doing to be supportive of the CEO?

4. What does the board need to know in order to assess organizational success in achieving financial and programmatic goals?

To what extent is the board aware of and knowledgeable about the organization's financial and programmatic success? What does the board know? What more does it need to know?

5. Are board meetings focused on the key strategic issues?

How was meeting time spent in the past year? What issues were addressed? What decisions were made?

6. Do committees have a clearly defined role?

What was each board committee's role and achievements in the past year?

well as donors. For example, an art museum that caters only to a narrow interest group will find its attendance waning as the demographics of communities change. Additionally, community foundations are now often inclined to fund exhibits designed to reach new audiences—young people from urban communities, for example. Furthermore, wealthy donors are no longer limited to the old guard; new entrepreneurs from diverse communities are becoming generous benefactors of arts organizations. Only boards that adapt their practices to this new environment will be effective in serving nonprofits and their important causes.

Good governance never happens by accident, only by design. The governance committee can play a role in ensuring board effectiveness on an ongoing basis by looking at board composition, recruitment, education, participation, assessment procedures, and structure.

Realigning Board Composition

Once the board has established a logical governance structure to focus on key organizational matters, the board can determine the kinds of experience, expertise, diversity, and relationships new members need to bring to the board. A useful approach to determine the best board composition is for the governance committee to lay out a grid of board committees; then list the skills, expertise, diversity, and relationships needed on each committee; then list the board members who already bring the needed qualifications to each committee; and, finally, identify the gaps in expertise for each committee. See Worksheet 6.4 for an example of such a grid. This exercise readily reveals the talents and experience that the board needs. For example, the development committee needs individuals who have experience in foundation giving, private giving, strategic planning, communications, and public relations. By plugging in board members who have such skills and then identifying gaps, the governance committee can ascertain the expertise that is lacking on the development committee and can find candidates who can supply that expertise. Because the chief executive has the best grasp of key issues on the horizon and the kinds of people who can add the greatest value, the governance committee should work in close concert with the chief executive to identify and recruit new members.

Having analyzed board composition, the governance committee, with the chief executive, can use Worksheet 6.5 to create a wish list of potential board members and a plan to identify and recruit individuals with the necessary backgrounds. In recruiting each new board candidate, the governance committee can then articulate its hopes and expectations regarding the new board member's involvement. Candidates appreciate learning how they can contribute and the expectations of them; people become enthusiastic about participating when they feel they can be useful, and they are impressed when the board has given thought to board-member recruitment.

It is important to create board openings by rotating in at least one new board member for every five board members every year. Boards that are stagnant lose the ability to see themselves or the organization with critical eyes. They become comfortable with the status quo, and they are often unable to recognize or accept opportunities for innovation. In today's dynamic environment, a board that is stuck in its habits will not be able to address challenges or maximize the organization's potential. In contrast, a carefully paced inflow of well-qualified new board members will bring fresh perspectives that will rejuvenate an organization and keep its mission and strategies relevant and effective.

There has been much debate about whether term limits are necessary in order to facilitate board-member rotation. Terms of three years are fairly common, and, for most organizations, that is the right amount of time to learn about the organization and to make a meaningful contribution. The controversy revolves around limiting board members to two or three three-year terms.

In the abstract, term limits should not be necessary in order to

Worksheet 6.4. Proposed Committee Composition.

	Executive Committee	Audit Committee	Finance Committee	Governance Committee	Development Committee	Communications Committee
	Size: Board officers and committee chairs	Size: 3–4 members	Size: 2–3 members	Size: 5 members	Size: 10 members	Size: 5 members
Expertise Sought:		• Accounting • Finance • Law	• Accounting • Finance • Investments • Law	• Nonprofit governance • Access to board-member prospects with fundraising potential • Access to diverse candidate prospects • Relationships in business community	• Corporate giving • Foundation giving • Private philanthropy • Public relations • Fundraising • Strategic planning • Public funding • Communications	• Marketing • Public relations • Communications • Media relations • Education • Strategic planning
Current Committee Members:		Chaired by Treasurer				
Gaps Identified:						

Worksheet 6.5. Building Your Board.

Expertise and Backgrounds Needed	Expertise and Backgrounds Already Available	Goals
Skills needed to strengthen the organization (e.g., public relations, finance, law, human resources, strategic planning) _____ _____ _____	Extent to which these skills exist among current board members _____ _____ _____	Goals to seek candidates with certain skills _____ _____ _____
Relationships needed for outreach/support/resources (e.g., segments of the business community) _____ _____ _____	Extent to which current board members have these relationships _____ _____ _____	Goals to seek candidates with certain relationships _____ _____ _____
Diversity needed for outreach/perspectives (e.g., women, African Americans, Hispanics/Latinos) _____ _____ _____	Extent to which diversity exists among current board members _____ _____ _____	Goals to seek candidates of certain races, ethnic origins, geographical locations, genders _____ _____ _____

gain the resignations of board members who are past their prime in serving the board, nor should term limits be necessary in order to create board vacancies. A healthy rotation system can be created by setting a basic understanding that most board members will serve two three-year terms; if this standard is a general practice, and not a rule in the by-laws, then exceptions can be made when necessary to retain an unusually valuable board member.

Furthermore, if boards are in fact determining the skills, expertise, diversity, and relationships that are needed on the board, then these qualifications should be the main determinants in deciding whether to renew a board member at the conclusion of each three-year term. In considering a board member for renewal, the governance committee should consider the values that the board member brings to the table in light of the organization's key strategic issues, while also considering the commitment that the board member has shown to the organization. Thus, term limits are not necessary when boards are functioning well, with clear expectations and accountability, as well as a process to assess board-member involvement and value.

In the abstract the arguments against term limits are persuasive. In practice, however, boards have shown that they lack the discipline to make the decision not to renew a board member, especially someone who is a friend or someone who has stature in the community. Even when board members are not contributing to the organization according to the board's standards, boards are loath not to invite them back for additional terms. Under such circumstances, term limits are the only solution because they allow for graceful exits. Those who argue for term limits suggest that if a board wants to renew a member for an additional term, the board can simply suggest that the board member leave the board for a year or serve on a board committee and then return. This common practice softens the strictures of term limits.

Perhaps the most compelling reason to adopt term limits is that boards that do not rotate members at a meaningful pace get stuck in outdated visions of the organization. One frequently hears such statements as "We tried that once and it didn't work" or "That is not what was intended when we founded the organization fifteen years ago." Furthermore, boards that retain members too long wind up with a hierarchy that reinforces the power of the longer-term members and discourages new views. There is a value in capturing institutional memory and history. Yet that goal can be achieved in ways other than to retain board members for unlimited terms; historical perspectives can be explored by a review of past minutes and interviews with people who played important roles in the organization's past—prior board chairs, chief executives, and even founding members. In today's dynamic environment, it is vital to rotate board members so that boards have fresh and diverse perspectives in leading organizations forward. In reality, boards that argue that they cannot afford to lose key members or that they have no candidates of the caliber needed are simply not doing their work in identifying and cultivating new candidates and building new relationships.

The Bottom Line

In order to leverage board members' time, experience, and commitment, first organize the board in a logical way and then add qualified new members.

7

Building Better Boards
Focus, Focus, Focus

This assembly [the First Continental Congress] is like no other that ever existed. Every man in it is a great man—an orator, a critic, a statesman, and therefore every man upon every question must show his oratory, his criticism, and his political abilities. . . . The consequence of this is that business is drawn and spun to immeasurable length. I believe if it was moved and seconded that we should come to a resolution that three and two make five, we should be entertained with logic and rhetoric, law, history, politics, and mathematics concerning the subject for two whole days, and then we should pass the resolution unanimously in the affirmative.

—John Adams, quoted in
D. McCullough, John Adams, 2001

Two of the most precious resources that board members bring to an organization are time and expertise. When board members' attention is focused on key organizational issues, their time and expertise are leveraged for the maximum benefit of the organization.

Board Meetings

Board meetings provide the occasion to focus the board's attention on the matters of utmost concern and to call the board to action accordingly. Examples of issues of appropriate magnitude for board meetings are the realignment of the organization's revenue model based on changes in funding patterns, a new resource-development plan, a community-relations and outreach strategy, an assessment of options for strategic alliances, a model to measure organizational outcomes, a plan to restructure the board for increased efficiency. Board members should leave each meeting with a renewed appreciation of the mission, an increased understanding of the challenges and opportunities facing the organization, a chance to have contributed to a discussion of importance, and the inspiration and direction to help the organization.

There is an art and a science to creating relevant and useful board meetings. The board chair and chief executive should develop the agenda together two to three weeks in advance of the board meeting. The agenda should focus on one or two key organizational issues and provide an opportunity for full board discussion. In this way, the board's limited time can be devoted to the issues that matter the most. Although the board chair sets the agenda, the chief executive can educate the chair about the most pressing organizational matters and ways in which the board can add value. Because the chief executive is the expert on issues related to funding, finances, and key programs and services, he or she should engage the board chair in a discussion of the issues that matter most and provide input and guidance regarding the content of the board meeting.

The chief executive should send the agenda and related materials to board members about ten days in advance of the meeting, in time for them to review the information and give some thought to the issues. Meeting materials should be clear, concise, and directly related to key issues. The focal point of the meeting should be an organizational matter that has been studied by the executive committee or a board committee in conjunction with the chief executive and staff. Preparation of this nature ensures that the board's precious time will be used productively.

The board chair should play the most important role in the meeting by involving all members in the discussion, keeping the meeting focused, and bringing the meeting to a close with a clear plan for next steps. As each major discussion ends, the board chair should make a judgment about whether to call for consensus or a vote, or to move the issue back to a board committee, ad hoc committee, executive committee, or staff for further discussion. The board chair must find the right balance to ensure forward momentum without pushing the board too aggressively. If a decision must be made within a certain time frame, the board chair needs to state how the matter will be concluded. The board chair should respect process while not allowing important issues to get bogged down because of the unreasonable demands of some board members. The chief executive should be the board chair's most valuable partner at the board meeting. Together, the board chair and the chief executive can gauge the right balance of speed and caution in the decision-making processes.

Meeting management is a major and difficult role for the board chair. For example, a board member may hijack a meeting in order to address a lesser matter or to undermine the chief executive. This distraction from more important business is destructive. The board chair must have the courage to state that she or he will be glad to discuss the concern further in private following the meeting and then must bring the agenda back into focus. The board chair must also ensure that discussions are respectful. For example, people on boards who are frustrated because they are not getting enough attention for minor matters sometimes make personal attacks on or criticize individuals on the board. The board chair must set the example and make expectations regarding interpersonal dynamics clear. Problem board members usually have to be dealt with one-on-one by the board chair and often need to be removed from the board. Board chairs who lack the courage to do so are only harming the organization; quality board members will not stay on boards that are dysfunctional because of runaway agendas and problem personalities.

In bringing a meeting to a close, the board chair should call for the board to engage in supportive activities such as fundraising and advocacy. For example, if an upcoming ballot issue will have serious implications for public funding for the organization, the board chair should call on board members to be knowledgeable about the issue, participate in meetings with people of influence, and attend community events.

Board members are highly sensitive to the rapport between the chief executive and the board chair. If they are working in harmony, board members are more likely to lend their support by giving time, expertise, and funds and by making introductions. When board members see tension between the board chair and the chief executive, they become concerned and hold back their support. Thus, for the sake of the organization the board chair and chief executive must work as partners and address any tensions that exist between them.

Finally, the board should receive minutes of all board meetings and key committee meetings. Board minutes should be drafted by a staff member under the guidance of the chief executive, but they need to be reviewed and finalized by the board secretary and then fully approved by the board at its next meeting. Committee-meeting minutes need to be reviewed and approved by the committee chair. Minutes provide an essential record and reference. They should capture the major issues discussed, key perspectives, and a record of any actions by the board. Minutes should also include a list of attendees as well as those absent, the date and location of the meeting, and the time the meeting was convened and adjourned. Minutes tell a great deal about the board, including the level of attendance, the relevance of the matters that were addressed, and the results of votes. In fact, by reviewing the minutes, one can assess the board's effectiveness. The minutes also provide the history of the organization. This record is necessary for accountability and is useful in understanding the past and planning for the future.

Involving Key Supporters in Nongoverning Capacities

Boards need to find a fitting and honorable role for people who are supportive of the nonprofit but who are not appropriate for the board. For example, some donors believe in the mission and the organization but do not have the time to attend board meetings. Other supporters do not have the expertise or background that the board is seeking at a given time. The chief executive, together with the board chair, should explore a variety of ways to involve and recognize such people.

One method is to establish an honorary status for major donors or longstanding supporters. Honorary board members can be invited to a special annual program as well as to other events. In addition, boards can consider establishing auxiliary bodies such as advisory councils, associate boards, and junior boards. Advisory and associate boards can comprise individuals who provide particular expertise or support—such as help with media relations or legal issues—on special occasions or as needed. It might not be necessary for these groups to meet, but the members should be recognized and appreciated.

Many organizations are now forming junior boards in order to involve younger supporters (usually people in their twenties and perhaps early thirties). Junior boards often play a role in friend-raising and fundraising, sometimes organizing gatherings of their peers to engage their interest and support. Members of junior boards can be invited onto the board after they have shown their commitment and value to the organization.

The one caveat with regard to advisory councils, associate boards, and junior boards is that they need to have a clearly stated purpose that unequivocally distinguishes their role from that of the board. Auxiliary groups should never be confused with the governing board. Tensions arise when auxiliary groups mistake their purpose as devising strategy or providing oversight. Furthermore, good staff support is necessary for an auxiliary body to be effective, so the organization needs to evaluate the costs and benefits of establishing additional groups.

Taking the Board to the Next Level

Sometimes organizations outgrow their boards. Sometimes the board members who founded an organization or even led the nonprofit through a stage of critical development are not the right people to govern the organization for the future. Take the example of an organization that suddenly receives a dramatic increase in funding because its mission has become the top priority for public funding or a large foundation. When an organization's budget goes from $250,000 to $3 million (yes, it can happen!), the organization will need to move from the small, grassroots level to a higher level of staffing, structure, funding, and accountability. The board members, and even the executive director, who had the vision to create the organization might not have the expertise, diversity, or relationships to advance the organization through this new period of growth and development.

In such a case, one or two key players—the chief executive, the board chair, a couple of board members, or one or two key funders—need to take responsibility for facilitating the re-creation of the board and possibly for engaging a new chief executive. The people who serve as the change agents can accelerate the process and make it less traumatic by hiring an outside consultant. The chair of one board that was in this situation said, "I want to create a board I couldn't get onto." This board chair did the organization a service by helping to engage new leadership, at the same time ushering out board members along with himself.

Although it is difficult for board members to let go and difficult for boards to recognize when they need to reinvent themselves, they need to contemplate their own relevance when changes occur in an organization's role and stature in the community. How will they know that the organization has outgrown the board? One indicator is the board's inability to address key strategic issues. Financial distress is another red flag. Who will know when this is the case? A small group of board members, and perhaps a funder or two, may have the insight and candor to raise the issue. In many cases, the chief executive sees that the organization has outgrown the board. In that case, the chief executive can plant the idea with a couple of board members or funders, but the chief executive is usually not in a position to facilitate the change, certainly not alone. How can a small group of board members, and possibly funders, bring about change? They need to underscore the key strategic issues and the implications for the future of the organization, such as potential decline or irrelevance, or new opportunities for expansion or renewal. Then they need to discuss the kind of board members who will be most useful to the organization in facing these challenges.

A board that hangs on and prevents the nonprofit from facing its key issues is strangling the organization and its opportunity to serve. A small band of courageous board members can bring about change. Facilitating change is a serious commitment, but its rewards can be tremendous. Board members who take the time and effort to build and advance an organization have the satisfaction of knowing they have rescued, expanded, or updated the organization in order to better serve the community.

The Role of Leaders in Keeping Boards Focused

The greatest challenge to leaders is leading board development in order to keep the board focused on priority issues. Although an improved structure might be possible in theory, groups often have difficulty adjusting to change, especially organizations that are deeply entrenched in decades of traditions and habits. These situations truly test leaders.

Board leaders must rise to the challenge of facilitating change for the sake of the communities they serve. Board leaders are most effective when they work in close collaboration with the nonprofit's chief executive in effecting progress. Reasonable board members understand the importance of adapting to contemporary challenges. Others, however, resist change no matter how compelling the reasons. In those cases, board leaders have to make tough decisions and move forward without the members who refuse to adapt. It helps when board leaders have a few other board members willing to collaborate to address the challenges.

The success of an organization in changing in order to remain focused depends on the effectiveness of the chief executive and the board chair. The next chapter addresses the qualities necessary to lead nonprofits in today's dynamic environment.

The Bottom Line

To leverage the board's time, it is necessary to focus on the big agenda to advance the organization. When the chief executive and board chair lead the board in identifying and addressing the key strategic issues, then the board can strengthen the organization in its mission to serve the community.

8

Strengthening Leadership

*A conductor's authority rests on two things: the
orchestra's confidence in the conductor's insightful
knowledge of the whole score; and the orchestra's faith
in the conductor's good heart, which seeks to inspire
everyone to make music that is excellent, generous,
and sincere.*
        —Michael Tilson Thomas, "Leading by Feel," 2004

Although nonprofit boards comprise an array of people who have various degrees of interest in the mission of the organization, the aggregate of their experience, expertise, and access to resources can strengthen the organization. The role of the board chair and the chief executive is to rally the board members to contribute their collective talents to achieve the organization's fullest potential.

Boards require capable leadership from the chair and from the chief executive. Chief executives need strong and capable boards in order to achieve organizational excellence. At the same time, board leaders need strong and capable chief executives. Optimal organizational outcomes can be achieved only with excellent leadership at the board and CEO levels.

Because board members are volunteers, the board chair must lead by providing inspiration, motivation, direction, coherence, and recognition. Board leaders must build consensus, energy, and excitement for the organization's purpose and future. The board chair leads by example, passion, reason, fairness, and respect for others. The position also requires courage because leaders must ultimately make sure that decisions are made in a timely manner, sometimes even without complete consensus.

The chief executive should be the top expert in all organizational matters and thus should facilitate the board's effectiveness by providing relevant information regarding the community's needs, the capacity of the organization, and its potential. The chief executive should lay out the key strategic and revenue opportunities for the board's consideration. Additionally, the chief executive should alert the board about threats to the organization's financial health, as well as alternative solutions to these challenges.

The Need for Integrity, Imagination, and Planning

The two most vital characteristics of effective leaders are integrity and imagination. Integrity is fundamental, the essential building block. People trust and follow leaders with integrity. Communities trust and fund organizations that are led by people with integrity. Integrity means honesty in all matters and genuine caring. Organizations and leaders with integrity can be counted on to be open and accountable.

Beyond integrity, leaders need imagination, of which there is an unfortunate shortage. Too many people are accustomed to seeing only the issues of the moment. Imagination is the ability to envision a better future and believe it is attainable. The role of the board chair, the chief executive, and the entire board is to imagine. To begin, the chief executive needs to make sure the board has a solid understanding of the mission and the major environmental forces that impinge on the mission. Then, the chief executive and board chair need to engage the board in envisioning a better future for the organization and for the community.

In a remote, rural community, the mission of an organization was to serve women who needed alcohol and drug treatment and protection from domestic violence but who resisted seeking help because of a deep cultural bias against sharing personal troubles outside the home. The executive director of the organization imagined an extraordinary solution. She persuaded someone to donate a lovely little house, and then she drew fearful women to the site by offering knitting and cooking classes; soon, women came to the house to knit and sew and to discuss their problems with alcohol, drugs, and domestic violence. This house became a safe haven for the women. The executive director then engaged treatment providers to come to the house to meet with the women and give them help.

As the demands on the organization grew, it was unable to draw sufficient funding from a community with increasingly limited resources. So the board had to imagine how it would sustain the services that were so needed and so useful. A local foundation engaged Business Volunteers Unlimited (BVU) to provide fresh insight, not in order to keep the organization alive, but to keep the services available to the women. The solution the group imagined and realized was to integrate the organization's services with those of a larger institution that provided a wide range of mental health and addiction services. Because the board comprised four women whose allegiance to the organization was based on their personal appreciation for its value rather than their business expertise, BVU also identified a new board member for the nonprofit—someone who had the experience to negotiate with the larger, new host institution—as well as funders whose financial support would continue to be necessary. The mission was accomplished. The larger institution adopted the program, and the funders are supporting these vital services in a new and stable home institution. The little house is still there to draw women into sewing and knitting classes where they share their troubles. This is an example of imagination—in conceiving of services to meet a need and then, eventually, in finding a permanent and sustainable home for the services.

Another example is a private school for inner-city children, more than half of whom are from families that live under the poverty line. As a result of the founders' belief that providing an academically intensive, communal environment for the children would be beneficial, the students' ability to succeed in state exams now far surpasses that of public school students. With the leadership of the principal and the board chair, a former vice chair at KeyCorp, who was placed on the board by a board-matching process, the school is completing a $16 million capital campaign to build a new facility and expand its programs.

Beyond imagining, the organization's chief executive needs to research and develop a solid plan to achieve the vision. The way to build a strong plan is to leverage the expertise of board members. The role of the board is to make sure that there is a clear plan with goals, aspirations, and potential funding sources; to do all they can to support the chief executive in achieving success; and to monitor progress toward goals. According to Susanna Lachs Adler, who has served in leadership roles on the boards of universities, independent schools, social service organizations, and other charities in the Philadelphia area, "The organizations that succeed have strong and capable chief executives and a well-thought-out mission statement. . . . The board must ensure that the leader has vision and the skills to implement the mission" (interview, July 21, 2004). Board leaders need to leverage members' energy and talents to achieve success. Once the chief executive and the board imagine the future and commit to a viable plan, the board must ask, "How can we help?" With imagination, good planning, and hard work, nonprofit organizations can strengthen health and human services, cultural centers, education, and civic and economic development. Exhibit 8.1 outlines board and CEO responsibilities for leadership and accountability.

Exhibit 8.1. The Board-CEO Pact.

The CEO Will	*The Board Will*

1. Shape the Mission, Vision, Strategic Direction
- Using careful assessments of community needs, organizational capacities, and funding potential as a foundation
- Drawing on the board's input through board and committee discussions and individual interviews
- Drawing on the input of key stakeholders

2. Be Accountable to the Board
- Providing programmatic information that shows results and outcomes
- Providing financial information that shows sound financial practices, results, and, if necessary, remedies

3. Lead the Organization
- Building a capable staff
- Developing resources with the board's full support
- Achieving the mission

1. Support the CEO
- Recognizing successes
- Providing appropriate compensation
- Interacting in a positive and constructive manner
- Allowing the CEO to lead the staff without interference
- Providing access to coaching, training, and consulting as needed

2. Focus on Key Organizational Opportunities and Challenges
- Understanding the organization's revenue model
- Understanding the key issues for organizational success
- Spending board meeting time on key matters

3. Provide Expertise and Insight
- Conversing on a one-on-one basis, in committee meetings, and at board meetings to help the CEO shape the mission, vision, and strategic direction

4. Help the CEO Achieve Organizational Success
- Making contributions, raising funds, advocating for the organization, providing expertise, and attending meetings

5. Hold the CEO Accountable
- Expecting financial and programmatic success
- Expecting remedies for challenges and strategies for taking advantage of opportunities

Choosing the Board Chair

Identifying and engaging the right person at the right time to chair the board is essential for organizational success.

The Process

Too often, board chairs rise to the position by default or some other random circumstance. Just as the recruitment of board members has traditionally been fairly random, so has the ascent to board leadership. Someone who is willing to serve, especially someone who is affable and well respected, is often installed as board chair even if she or he does not have the requisite experience or qualifications. Even worse, sometimes board members of means or stature can bully their way into leadership positions, even though most board members know that they are not suitable candidates. It is a serious problem that the ascent to board leadership is so poorly managed even though the caliber of board leadership is probably the most powerful factor in organizational success. In today's challenging conditions, this haphazard approach can lead to the organization's demise. Boards must define the role of the chair, determine the qualifications needed, and establish a thoughtful process to identify, groom, and engage the chair.

The role of the board governance committee is to work in collaboration with the chief executive to develop the slate of board officers, including the board chair. The governance committee should present the slate of officers—board chair, vice chair(s), treasurer, and secretary—to the board for election at the annual meeting, an occasion that is set according to the organization's by-laws.

The qualifications that are most important depend on the organization and its key issues. For example, a grassroots organization may need a leader who can raise the organization to its next stage of development by attracting board members who are respected by key constituents and who bring strategic vision and business skills. However, a well-established and traditional organization may need a leader who represents the next generation in order to engage a broader and younger constituency that will ensure the organization's long-term viability. Again, an organization that sees charitable support diminishing may need a leader who recognizes the importance of developing new revenue models. In another case, an organization that has a reputation for being exclusive and isolated may seek a board leader who represents a more inclusive approach. A board needs to consider the organization's strengths and future potential in order to find the type of leader who can advance the organization to the next stage. Candidates for board chair need to have demonstrated their commitment to the mission and the organization through prior participation. A perfect way to learn about the leadership ability of board members is to involve prospective board chairs as committee chairs and officers. The board then has a chance to see them in action, and at the same time people with potential can become better acquainted with the organization.

The board governance committee should consider the chief executive's input in identifying the board chair. The chief executive has the best knowledge of each board member's involvement and commitment. Furthermore, it is in the organization's best interest to have a board chair who works well with the chief executive. That partnership relationship is central to organizational success. As noted in Chapter Seven, board members are attuned to the relationship between the board chair and the chief executive, and their perception of that relationship can affect their participation on the board.

Succession planning is necessary to create a pipeline of viable board leaders. When potential leaders serve as committee chairs and officers, the organization has a continuous flow of people who are tested in action. This practice also protects the organization from having no one to replace leaders who move away for professional or personal reasons. Another reason to develop a pool of future leaders is that as organizations evolve, the kind of board chairs they need varies. When the governing committee assesses the candidates who might succeed to leadership, the committee needs to imagine the organization as it will be in the future. For example, after a period of rapid transition and transformation, the organization may need a solid, credible, and well-respected business leader who projects strength and stability. But an organization that has been criticized for being staid and unwilling to adapt to a new era may be better served by a board chair who is less traditional—perhaps an entre-preneurial, small-business owner—and who projects openness, change, progress, and innovation.

Qualities of an Effective Board Chair

Boards and chief executives need to consider a number of charac-teristics when recruiting the board chair or planning for succession.

Personal Qualities

As already discussed, good board chairs have integrity. Their word is trusted, and they are recognized for their true commitment to the well-being of the community.

A good board chair also has a keen intellect, the courage to lead, and the ability to inspire people, make good judgments, and develop consensus. Nonprofit organizations face complex chal-lenges in establishing their relevance, developing new revenue models, focusing on services with demonstrable results, and docu-menting and communicating their compelling value. This is not a job for those who are faint of heart or modest of intellect. A good board chair is a seasoned and skilled facilitator, negotiator, and advocate.

Board chairs must have a realistic notion of the amount of work and responsibility involved in leading an organization, treat others with respect, be open to new ideas, and be able to make tough deci-sions. They must be able to synthesize information and input in order to identify the key issues and sort out the less important dis-tractions. They must be able to recognize the issues that matter most and stay focused in moving the organization forward. Most important, they must work in close collaboration with the chief executive, recognizing the depth of her or his expertise and commitment to organizational success.

Concern for the Organization and Its Mission

To be effective, a board chair must genuinely care about the mission, the organization, and most important, the community. Board members, funders, and staff members rally behind a leader who cares. Along with members of the public, they see through a leader who is using the organization for career advancement, ego, or self-aggrandizement, and who, as a result, does not work hard on behalf of the organization.

Grasp of the Issues and of the Broad Context

A good board chair must understand the work of the organization as well as the broader context. Management gurus Rosabeth Moss Kanter (1995) and Peter Drucker (2000) claim that the challenges facing nonprofits are tougher than the most complex challenges facing businesses.

Board chairs need to work with chief executives to encourage the board to give major attention to key organizational issues; chairs needs to make sure that they and their boards are getting the information they need from the chief executive and external sources in order to gauge the organization's relevance, effectiveness, and financial health. Most important, board chairs need to have a vision of organizational success that is consistent with that of the chief executive and to engage the board in helping to achieve that vision.

Ability to Facilitate Meetings

The board chair must be an excellent meeting facilitator, particularly because the board meeting is the occasion when board members give their combined attention to the organization. A productive board meeting begins with the creation of a good agenda, which should be developed by the board chair in consultation with the chief executive. Together, they need to design a meeting that focuses the board's attention on key organizational issues, provides an opportunity for discussion, and calls for board-member participation in supporting the organization. People are on boards because they want to make a contribution. They need direction in understanding how they can add value. They look to leaders for focus and clarity.

Perhaps the most important role of the board chair is to focus the board's full attention on a vision of organizational success. Unfortunately, boards are easily distracted by less important matters. Furthermore, some board members are threatened by change, and they distract the board from looking and advancing forward.

> Focusing your attention on the most clamorous of your followers will not only anger and alienate the healthier among them. It will distract you from working with the entire group on what actually matters, accomplishing a common mission. Knowing *what* to pay attention to is just as important and just as difficult. In their efforts to effect changes, leaders coming into new organizations are often thwarted by an unconscious conspiracy to preserve the status quo. Problem after problem will be dumped in your lap—plenty of new ones and a bulging archive of issues left unresolved by previous administrators—and responding to them all ensures that you will never have time to pursue your own agenda [Thomas, 2004, p. 27].

Sometimes a board member distracts the board by focusing on a pet project that is not especially consequential. In other cases, board members may distract board attention merely to compensate for issues in their personal lives, such as retirement from a high-status job. In other cases, board members with particular expertise, such as finance, get carried away in a detailed review of accounts payable rather than allowing the board to focus on the overall financial report and its implications. Or board members may be "stuck in time," perceiving the nonprofit as it was a decade or two earlier. Such board members are inhospitable to change and progress. In these cases, the board chair must play a leadership role in meetings and in preparation for and follow-up to meetings, to make sure that board members who are moving the discussions astray are handled firmly but respectfully.

The board chair must lead the board in imagining the potential for the organization, staying focused on the opportunities, and dealing with the challenges. By setting meeting agendas that are devoted to matters of consequence and keeping the discussion on track, the board chair can ensure that the board's limited time and attention are leveraged to the advantage of the organization.

Each board meeting should provide the time and space for board members to deliberate about the vital issues that can either inhibit or advance the organization. If issues need to be voted on, board members should have all the relevant information at hand to make good decisions. Appropriate information should be sent to board members more than a week in advance; the information should be clear, concise, and focused.

Board meetings also provide a valuable opportunity for the board chair to role-model good participation. By recognizing and complimenting board members for particular contributions, the board chair is giving due honor while also indicating to other board members the contributions that are valued and how they are helpful.

Board members should leave each meeting having been inspired about the work of the organization, having a deeper understanding of key organizational challenges and opportunities, having had an opportunity to make a contribution to the discussion, and having clear ideas about how they can support the organization as a board and as individuals.

Board Officers and Committee Chairs

Effective board leadership cannot be the responsibility of the chair alone. A small, core group of board leaders needs to support the chair. By engaging competent individuals as vice chair, treasurer, and secretary, the board forms a team of capable people with complementary skills and qualities. An additional advantage to this model is having potential chair successors among the board officers. Although the governance committee has the responsibility for forming the slate of officers for nomination to the board, the committee should consult with the chair candidate and the chief executive for their input. A leadership team with good chemistry will be most productive. Team members do not need to agree at all times, but they do need to show respect for each other and share a serious commitment to the organization.

In most organizations, officers are nominated by the governance committee and elected by the board, usually at the board's annual meeting. The governance committee should prepare the slate after carefully considering the skills and qualities that the organization needs in its leaders and meeting with officer candidates to ascertain their interest and availability.

Vice Chairs

The board can install one, two, or three vice chairs. In some cases, it is helpful to have clarity about leadership succession by publicly identifying the successor to the board chair. In such instances, the vice chair can be designated as the chair-elect, or the board can simply name someone as chair-elect. However, having two or three vice chairs gives the board more options and broadens the base of leadership and talent. There are pros and cons to lining up successors. When there is a logical and highly qualified candidate to succeed the chair, it is helpful to plan ahead and provide an opportunity for the successor to prepare through participation as a vice chair, especially in complex nonprofits. However, by identifying the successor a year or two in advance, an organization can lock itself into a situation it may later come to regret if the candidate proves to be less worthy than anticipated or if the key organizational issues shift and a different skill set is required in the next board chair. These are issues to be discussed by the board governance committee.

Secretary

The secretary should be an attorney because he or she needs to have a good understanding of the board's fiduciary responsibility as well as the organization's public accountability. The secretary is responsible for the meeting minutes, although the minutes can be drafted by a staff person and then reviewed and finalized by the secretary. The secretary is the keeper of organizational records as required by law.

Treasurer

The treasurer should have a financial background and a basic understanding of nonprofit accounting. The treasurer works with the organization's chief executive and chief financial officer. Together with the finance committee, which the treasurer should chair, the treasurer should recommend an auditor to the board, meet with the auditor in advance of the annual audit, and meet with the auditor at the completion of the audit. The treasurer should review the organization's financial reports as prepared by the senior financial staff person at least quarterly and should present them to the board, as well as raise questions about the organization's revenues, expenses, and investments.

Committee Chairs

Committee chairs are vital for board effectiveness. Committees should be created based on organizational priorities (see Chapter Five). Each committee should have a clear charge and comprise board members who bring specific skills, expertise, and relationships to the table; in some cases, it is appropriate to add non-board members in order to fill gaps in talent. Each committee needs a chair who has a clear understanding of the work of the committee and how it relates to larger organizational strategy. The committee chairs should work with the chief executive to make sure the committee's work is conducted within the broad strategic framework, to establish meeting schedules and agendas, and to ensure that committee members have the information they need and that the committee fulfills its role productively and efficiently. Each committee chair should report on the committee's work to the board and also have a seat on the executive committee in order to ensure a collaborative effort. In larger nonprofits, the chief executive may designate a key staff person to work with each committee; in small organizations, that staff person might be the chief executive. The qualifications for committee chair are similar to those for the board chair; they include a commitment to the mission and community, a keen intellect, an ability to facilitate inclusive yet focused discussions, and a thoughtful respect for members of the board and staff.

Possible Chair-CEO Scenarios

The ability and style of the key leaders—the board chair and the chief executive—as well as their partnership relationship, can bring success to the organization or stymie it. Because each leader is relatively effective or ineffective, four combinations of leaders based on this characteristic are possible, as illustrated in Figure 8.1.

Scenario 1: Effective Chair, Effective Chief Executive

When an organization has an effective board chair and an effective chief executive, the organization is most likely providing high-quality services to the community, communicating its compelling value, maximizing revenue potential, and measuring and documenting its relevance, integrity, and financial health. Board members are engaged and contributing their talents, expertise, resources, and relationships. The board's capacity and attention are fully lever-

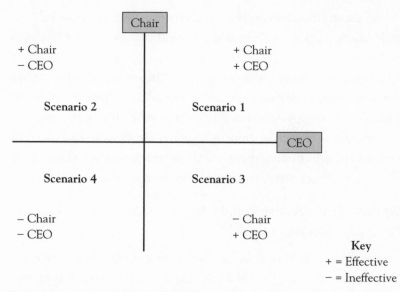

Figure 8.1. **Possible Chair-CEO Scenarios.**

aged. The organization's staff is performing at peak levels. The community is well served. This is the best-case situation.

Scenario 2: Effective Chair, Ineffective Chief Executive

Consider an organization in which an ineffective chief executive is weak in leading the executive team, uncomfortable raising money, and does not communicate with the board. The organization is not maximizing its revenues, the staff is not performing at peak effectiveness, and the board and chief executive are not working in concert.

In today's fiscal environment, the organization might rapidly go downhill. One possible remedy is for the board to engage paid or volunteer consultants to coach, train, and assist the chief executive. In the for-profit universe business executives have access to professional services; it is reasonable and often necessary to help nonprofit executives develop their abilities as well. (See the discussion of coaching and training below.)

When the chief executive is underperforming, the board should make its expectations clear, and it should provide regular feedback and guidance to facilitate the executive's professional development. If the executive is unable to improve within a reasonable time, then the board must seek a new executive to lead the organization. In the case of an ineffective chief executive, the problem can be remedied by installing an effective chair, who can assess the situation and the various options, discuss them with the board, and act accordingly. The board chair's attentiveness and intervention is key.

Scenario 3: Ineffective Board Chair, Effective Chief Executive

Imagine that a new board chair becomes anxious about the enormity of the responsibility of leading a multi-million-dollar organization that is under scrutiny by public authorities and the media because of the sensitive nature of the children's services that it provides. To add to the challenge, the organization's funding is jeopardized by new state funding priorities. The board chair responds to the stress by questioning the integrity of a seasoned and capable chief executive and conducting private meetings with board officers; as a result his relationship with the chief executive is tense and combative, and board members are being dragged into unpleasant politics and asked to take sides. The chief executive is already working under duress given the demands on the organization and is now diverting a great deal of energy to dealing with the board chair and new schisms within the board. She is distracted from fundraising, and she and her executive team are becoming demoralized. Under these adverse conditions, the organization is underperforming. In today's environment, the organization cannot endure this tension without its services and capacity being impaired.

There are no easy remedies. Only a well-established chief executive would dare challenge such a contentious board chair, and even then doing so would be risky. The only solution is for a few board members to facilitate a transition to a new board chair. At the same time, these board members need to bolster the chief executive in order to mitigate the damage caused by the board chair. In such instances, outside consultants and facilitators can be helpful in providing enlightened perspectives.

Scenario 4: Ineffective Board Chair, Ineffective Chief Executive

Consider an even worse situation. When an organization has an ineffective board chair and an ineffective chief executive, the board and the staff all become demoralized. Even good board members do not contribute because the situation presents neither the climate nor the opportunity for doing so. Board members start disappearing either by resigning or simply not coming to meetings.

Lacking leadership and direction, factions of the board are likely to be at odds with each other. Board meetings are unfocused, and board roles are confused and probably conflict with staff roles. Staff members are also frustrated and leave for better work environments. Funding is undermined; clients are not well served; the organization is in free fall.

Under these circumstances, there are only two possible remedies, both extreme. One is for a few board members to reach out to funders to seek their collaboration in replacing the board leadership, the chief executive, and possibly the entire board. This is usually a brutal process, and it takes great courage and tenacity. Alternatively, in the absence of any board-member initiative, a funding organization or two can act independently to replace the board leadership, the chief executive, and possibly the entire board. Board members are sometimes surprised that the funding community is aware of the organization's distress, yet, in most communities, perhaps with the exception of the largest cities, the nonprofit universe has few secrets.

The lesson learned from the four scenarios just described is that purposeful succession planning is imperative. Boards need to focus serious attention on identifying potential board leaders and involving them as committee chairs and officers so that their abilities and commitment can be tested. Boards must be thoughtful about the skills they need in a board chair, and they must develop and assess potential candidates. Nonprofit organizations cannot afford to have leaders move into key roles simply through happenstance. The succession process must be by design. Boards must accept the responsibility to identify, develop, and promote capable board leaders.

The Role of the Chief Executive vis-à-vis the Board

The situations just described indicate the interdependence of the chief executive and the board chair. For an organization to be effective nothing is more important than the relationship between the board chair and the chief executive. Friction between the two destabilizes the organization, undermines leadership morale, and bleeds over to the board and the staff. A mutually respectful and productive relationship, however, allows the organization to soar.

The nonprofit sector, especially organizations that receive significant community funding and resources, is increasing its expectations of its executives. Today's boards understand that passion alone in a chief executive is not sufficient and that time in the trenches does not translate into management ability. As boards begin to hire chief executives who are truly prepared to lead and manage, boards must also respect the chief executive's role. A board should not be involved in leading the staff, making management decisions, and developing and implementing organizational plans. Instead, the board should empower the executive while also holding her or him accountable. The board can exercise its oversight role by asking the chief executive for a dashboard of information that shows the organization's progress according to key indicators. The board should monitor qualitative and quantitative measures and call for remedies when key goals are not met. The role of the board chair is to leverage the energy and talents of board members and serve as the point person for the board's interaction with the chief executive. Consequently, the relationship between the board chair and the chief executive is the key to the entire organization's effectiveness.

It is incumbent on the chief executive to work at establishing rapport with the board chair. At the same time, the board chair must understand the stresses of running a nonprofit, develop insight into the nature of the enterprise, and help establish a positive rapport. Most important, the board chair needs to demonstrate care for the organization and its effectiveness and be willing to be a partner with the chief executive. Because communication between the board chair and the chief executive is of primary importance, they need to establish a format for ongoing discussion: perhaps a weekly phone appointment and a monthly or semimonthly meeting depending on the nature of the nonprofit enterprise and its challenges and on the style of the board chair and chief executive. They may have a structured, formal style or one that is more spontaneous. In any case, communication needs to be open and flexible. The chief executive should be able to call the board chair for input and counsel, while also having confidence that his or her role as chief executive will be respected. One board chair who was consulted for his advice on a management matter said to the chief executive, "Okay, since you ask, I'll give you my suggestions. But this one is your call since you are the chief executive." In such cases, the chief executive seeks the board chair's input based on respect for that person's intellect and insight, and the board chair is clear about the parameters of her or his role.

Sometimes conflicts occur when board and staff roles are confused. The tension can often be alleviated by defining the key governance issues. Good information, clearly presented, can also help ameliorate relationships between the board and staff; with appropriate and useful information, the board can focus its attention on the issues that matter most and make good decisions. Often an outside consultant or another board member can help provide a balanced perspective and diplomatic solution.

Board leaders need to make sure that boards recognize and appreciate the work and successes of nonprofit executives in helping organizations meet difficult challenges. Boards must establish appropriate compensation packages that are aligned with the organization's size, scope, and sophistication; commend executives for effectiveness; and make introductions to business and community leaders who can help the chief executive in leading the organization. CompassPoint, a leading nonprofit resource center based in San Francisco, produced a study entitled *Daring to Lead: Nonprofit Executive Directors and Their Work Experience* (Peters and Wolfred, 2001). The report underscores the importance of board support for the chief executive. "Clearly boards make a difference. The larger agencies appear to have boards who have more effectively teamed up with their executives. And executive tenure in agencies of all sizes seems to be impacted by the degree of perceived board support. . . . The data show that boards who don't monitor executive job satisfaction, including satisfaction with compensation, are likely to experience turnover. Board leadership should regularly consider not only the performance of their executives, but their levels of fatigue, stress, and frustration" (p. 32).

If the chief executive is not performing up to expectations, then the board leaders need to provide candid and constructive feedback and resources for coaching and training. If the chief executive is not able to fulfill the role even after coaching and guidance, the board must replace the chief executive. Boards should expect excellence from chief executives, and boards should recognize and appreciate high performance.

Some people believe that everyone is replaceable. Although good leaders can indeed be replaced with new good leaders, it is not easy to find people who are qualified and capable of effectively leading nonprofits. Stories abound of organizations that suffer miserably when a highly talented and visionary chief executive departs. Many organizations that lose their leaders fail fast and hard; some simply wither. But other organizations experience a renaissance with a new leader. So, although everyone may be replaceable, the person matters. Thus, boards need to cherish, support, and seek to retain outstanding chief executives. Chief executives, in turn, need to appreciate and support superior board chairs, who are also hard to find.

Evaluating Board Leaders

Boards routinely evaluate chief executives. This board responsibility should be performed annually with careful thought and attention (see Chapter Five on evaluating CEOs). Although the role of board chair and the roles of key board officers are as least as important as the role of the chief executive, however, there is no standard for assessing board leadership. Having an evaluation process for board officers would provide a number of benefits. First, devising the assessment tool would be in and of itself an educational process for clarifying the roles and expectations of key board leaders. Second, having an assessment would underscore the importance of the officers in bringing about organizational success. Third, an assessment would help board leaders consider how they could improve their effectiveness. Fourth, an assessment would provide a process through which leadership transitions could be facilitated. As noted above, ineffective board chairs can cripple an organization; they must be replaced in a timely fashion before the damage is serious.

Board officers should be asked to conduct an annual self-assessment of their understanding of the key issues facing the organization and their ability to focus the board's attention on the key issues; involve all board members in board discussions and activities; establish an effective rapport with the chief executive; support the creation of an effective revenue model that ensures organizational viability; lead the board in resource development; and ensure that there is accountability for the organization's results as well as remedies for weaknesses in performance. Worksheet 8.1 is an example of a form board chairs and other officers can use to assess their effectiveness as leaders.

Board officers should be asked to assess themselves on these abilities and share their thoughts in a meeting facilitated by a board consultant, with the chief executive present. The process provides an opportunity for board officers to reflect on their effectiveness, seek guidance, or, in some cases, step down. Self-assessment creates an expectation that board officers will perform well, understand and meet their fiduciary responsibilities, be thoughtful about their roles, and be accountable to their peers. A board-officer self-assessment is also a tool for prospective board leaders to use to evaluate their own interests and qualifications with regard to leadership positions.

Coaching, Mentoring, and Training

As we have seen, in today's nonprofit environment, the challenges and opportunities require high intellect, inventiveness, and the ability to problem-solve and lead. One is not born with fully developed leadership skills. Leaders can accelerate their learning by seeking guidance from others who have demonstrated their abilities. Board matchmakers, nonprofit resource centers, and board consultants have an opportunity to offer sophisticated services to train and coach board leaders as well as nonprofit executives. These services need to be provided by people who have demonstrated their capabilities in leadership roles. Coaches and trainers can be helpful to

Worksheet 8.1. Self-Assessment Form for Board Officers.

1. I can identify the organization's key strategic issues. They are as follows:

2. I am supportive of and helpful to the CEO in the following ways:

3. I articulate to the board and board members specifically how they can be helpful to the organization and the CEO in the following ways and on the following occasions:

4. I meet with the CEO, one-on-one, face-to-face, at least once per quarter to discuss key strategic issues and how the board and I can help. [Board chair: meetings may be monthly.]

5. I make sure that there is an adequate compensation package, positive feedback, and constructive support for the CEO. I engage other board leaders in ensuring this support as well. [Or, I have concerns about the CEO's performance, and I have done the following to bring about change:]

6. I receive and understand reports from the CEO regarding financial and programmatic success and outcomes as related to key organizational goals. When there are obstacles to success or failures to meet goals, I assist the CEO in determining remedies or suitable shifts in course. I ensure that the board understands these matters as well. Here are a few specific examples:

7. I address the compelling value of the organization in discussions with people of influence in the community. Here are a few examples:

8. [Chair only] I facilitate board meetings and executive committee meetings in a manner that keeps the board focused on the key organizational issues and ways in which board members can be helpful to the CEO. The majority of meeting time in the past year has been used to address the following issues:

9. I allow the CEO to lead the organization without interfering with staff hiring and management.

both paid and volunteer personnel. Experienced board leaders who are retired business or community leaders are often delighted to coach the next generation of leaders. There is often more art than science to volunteer leadership, so a wise counselor who has learned through trial and error can be a highly valuable resource.

Additionally, board leaders should be encouraged to reach out to people who might serve as mentors. A new board chair can seek the advice of the past board chair or of her or his boss at work or of a colleague who has experience in this arena. Board leaders should feel that asking for advice is not a sign of weakness, but rather a learning opportunity and a path to excellence and effectiveness. Warren Bennis, Distinguished Professor of Business Administration at the University of Southern California and author of more than twenty-five books on leadership and change, advises that "the best mentors are usually recruited, and one mark of a future leader is the ability to identify, woo, and win the mentors who will change his or her life" (2004, p. 46). Board leaders who are open to learning from those who are more experienced accelerate their personal development and become capable leaders.

The Democratization of Leadership

One of the most exciting and invigorating changes to occur in the nonprofit sector is the democratization of leadership. Until a decade ago, one could make a very short list of key business and community leaders in every city and realize that they and their cronies were heading every significant nonprofit board. They were all white, they had great wealth, they were mostly over fifty years old and often well over sixty, and they were almost all men or, occasionally, the wives or descendants of men who made money. These leadership volunteers are certainly to be credited for their commitment to the community and their limitless hours of service. Many could have enjoyed their lives without the bother of community service, but, instead, they chose to dedicate themselves and be generous.

The misfortune of the past leadership model is that it was exclusive; most community resources were controlled by a handful of people. Some people are wistful when they think of an era when communities could make strategic decisions and implement them simply by rounding up the small group of the elite. Although it may seem appealingly simple, this approach has become obsolete; a small, exclusive group of decision makers would be dreadfully out of touch with the needs and interests of communities that include people from many backgrounds and cultures.

Today's model may seem unwieldy, but it is a great advancement. Today, anyone who has the intellect, interest, and passion can lead a nonprofit by serving on the board as a member or an officer. In a single community, the two hundred largest nonprofits may be led by almost that many different board chairs. These board chairs may include women, younger adults in their thirties, African Americans, Latinos, Asian Americans, rich and poor. Furthermore, they may come from a variety of working worlds including the nonprofit, government, and academic arenas, as well as large and small businesses.

This seismic shift is the democratization of leadership: the leveraging of talent from all corners of the community and the contributions of many voices and perspectives in imagining and shaping the future. In the United States, 1.2 million nonprofits with close to seventeen million paid and volunteer workers provide vital and varied services in health and human services, the arts, education, environmental protection, and civic and economic development (Salamon, 1999, p. 22). This sector now has access to the talents and minds of a broad range of people based on their qualifications and their personal passions. This is a powerful situation!

For women and minority individuals, boards that are forward-looking can provide leadership development opportunities. The opportunity to engage such a wide variety of people makes it all the more important for matchmakers to link candidates with nonprofit boards based on qualifications and interests. By helping nonprofits access a diverse pool of excellent candidates, matchmakers can help organizations be increasingly responsive to community needs and interests and to reach new sources of support and funding. Organizations whose boards are inclusive have the greatest impact in serving a wide variety of people.

The Next Generation

One of the most important responsibilities of today's volunteer leaders is to encourage and develop the next generation of leaders. This cultivation can be achieved through a variety of leadership development organizations that are becoming prevalent (for example, many cities have leadership programs based at the chambers of commerce). Business leaders also need to seek out the young professionals in their companies, support their involvement on boards, and serve as role models and coaches. Now is the time to involve people in their twenties in "friends groups," advisory boards, and board committees, and to involve people in their thirties on boards and board committees so they can develop the experience required to move into leadership roles.

People develop leadership ability through the rigors of active experience. The learning process can be supported by training and coaching. Training should be offered by consultants and nonprofit resource centers. Coaching should be provided by experienced and well-respected board leaders as well as professional coaches and trainers. Leadership development cannot be left to chance. The success of communities will depend on the effectiveness of the next generation of leaders.

The Bottom Line

Leaders are visionaries who can energize and inspire others to contribute to a common purpose. Leadership needs to be developed and nurtured. Boards need to include people from a broad variety of backgrounds and younger adults, and individuals of talent and com-

mitment should be encouraged and supported in rising to leadership positions. Only then can the nonprofit sector achieve its fullest
potential in serving all citizens and building strong and healthy
communities.

The full force of a board can be leveraged by strong leaders. An
effective chief executive, in partnership with a capable and dedicated board chair, can maximize a board's potential to serve the
community's best interests.

9

Bold Vision and Iterative Planning

*What we will become depends entirely on our vision
and our will.*
—*Mario Vargas Llosa, "Why Literature?" 2002*

Although the challenges facing nonprofits are often daunting, and the tides of change are powerful, often the most successful nonprofit organizations are the ones with the boldest visions. An example is The Gathering Place, "a caring community that supports, educates and empowers individuals and families touched by cancer through programs and services provided free of charge" (annual report, 2003). The Gathering Place was established in 1999 by Eileen Saffran, who is its executive director. Only four years later, The Gathering Place had already provided services to over forty-five hundred individuals who visited the center for programs and assistance on over forty thousand occasions. It serves people from 255 zip codes, including twenty-seven states and six countries. In 2003, The Gathering Place raised close to $3 million (surpassing its $2 million campaign goal) to build, mortgage-free, a twelve thousand-square-foot facility to house its programs and services. The new facility also includes a magnificent landscape garden for discussion groups, children's activities, and simple strolls. Saffran explains the key success factors: there was a need to be filled as individuals and their families were challenged by the onslaught of cancer, and the

timing was right because health care providers, including tradi-
tionalists, were beginning to see the connection between mind and
body and thus the value of helping patients develop tools to cope
with their stress and anxieties (interview, 2004).

Saffran marshaled a grassroots effort, as well as the philanthropic
communities, around her vision. Within the first six months, the
initial planning group of twelve people had to move their meeting
site to an auditorium to accommodate all those interested in supporting the vision of a healing center for people touched by cancer.
Additionally, Saffran engaged Margo Roth to serve as chair of the
board. Margo has devoted herself to building a board that is highly
supportive and engaged in achieving the vision for The Gathering
Place. The existence of The Gathering Place is all the more impres-
sive given the hostile funding climate. It is proof that bold visions
can be achieved if there is a clear need, a strong case for support,
and a dynamic and unrelenting leader who knows how to build
broad-based support.

The nonprofit sector is highly dynamic. In the life of the chief
executive of a nonprofit organization, each quarter brings news of
a corporate funder dropping out because of market forces, a foundation that is shifting dollars to a new area, legislation that will
require a major change in service delivery, fresh demands for outcome measurement, and the unavoidable need for improved technology to track services for third-party reimbursement. Some days
bring better news, such as the emergence of a new funding source.
Other days bring developments that can be good or bad, such as the
departure of the board chair to another city or interest from a potential new organizational partner. In all such cases, serious work is
involved in mitigating a loss or leveraging an opportunity.

In such an environment, the only way for an organization to
thrive is to be nimble. The chief executive must have the intellect,
experience, flexibility, drive, passion, and diplomacy to reorient the
organization and the strategic plan. The chief executive must have
a senior team of highly talented, devoted, and flexible profession-

als who have the expertise to grasp the issues as they arise, the coordination to move in new directions, and the adaptability, camaraderie, and good humor to plow forward through new challenges on a regular basis.

Iterative Planning for a Dynamic Environment

The thought of strategic planning sends shudders through some people. They imagine a series of long, arduous, and mind-numbing meetings where too many people who know too little can talk for too long. Most strategic-planning processes involve an all-day retreat, often on a sunny weekend when nobody wants to be working. These large-scale events are usually designed to occur every few years. Despite the drawbacks, there are times in the life of an organization when a major time-out is warranted. For example, a large-scale planning effort may be necessary if there are significant or accumulated assaults on the revenue structure, a dramatic new funding opportunity, or a change in the organization's leadership. A large-scale strategic-planning effort can provide the occasion for the board and staff to gather and analyze the data and reorient the organization accordingly. It is usually helpful to have an outside facilitator guide such a process. It can also be useful to have outside researchers gather relevant information so that the staff is not distracted from its primary work. (Because most nonprofits do not have a cushion in regard to staff time and resources for the strategic-planning effort, it is worthwhile pursuing grant funding for the outside facilitator and researchers.)

However, an organization that conducts planning only every few years is guaranteed to become obsolete before it is time for a new strategic-planning event. Strategic planning is valuable as long as it is a dynamic process, not an event. In the best-led organizations, strategic planning is an iterative process that is built into the organizational fabric and fed by a steady flow of information. Only through iterative planning can an organization keep itself relevant, ensure high impact, maintain its viability, and thrive. A board of directors should expect the chief executive to establish a year-round, continuous planning effort. Indeed, this is the chief executive's most important job.

Imagine a sailboat embarking on a journey in the wide-open ocean. To begin, the skipper needs to establish a clear direction and path. With the help of the crew, the skipper fixes the boat's position, maps the course, and evaluates the seasonal tides and winds. They make sure that the boat is navigable in the environment. Nevertheless, although they have a plan, they need to adjust it on a continual basis depending on the weather, tides, and emerging conditions. Consequently, they need a group process for continuously gathering and assessing information and adjusting their course and strategies quickly and capably. They may need to trim their sails, change their heading, or shift the crew as ballast. The crew may even need to replot the course before adjusting the helm. A storm will require the crew to rely on landmarks or technology to fix their position; repairs may be needed as well. The crew has to be a group of skilled and experienced sailors who work well as a team and are committed to making the journey. They need to be nimble and well-practiced in order to adapt in a timely fashion, or they risk losing time, failing to reach the destination, or even sinking. Staying in place is not an option. Finally, the captain must be clearly in charge so that all activity is coordinated to achieve the common purpose and goal.

Like a ship's crew, a nonprofit organization has a skipper—the chief executive—and the nonprofit has a destination—the achievement of a vision. It must constantly assess the environment and adapt to changes in the winds and the tides in order to accomplish its mission. Failing to accurately gauge the elements and adjust course means sinking. With good leadership and a team of experts who read all the signals and adapt accordingly, the nonprofit will reach its goal.

The Iterative-Planning Process

Strategic planning should be woven into every aspect of organizational work, and it should be led by the chief executive. It should be the basis for daily decisions related to staffing, funding, the use of money (such as purchasing new software or hardware), and the use of time (such as attending certain meetings rather than others).

Mission Statement

The basis of an iterative strategic plan is a clearly defined mission—an enduring and compelling purpose. The mission statement provides an image of what the organization will be. Here are a few sample mission statements from nonprofit organizations:

> Camp Periwinkle: To rehabilitate the emotional well being of children with cancer and blood disorders through uplifting camp activities in a safe environment away from the hospital routine.

> Cleveland Public Theatre: To inspire, nurture, challenge, amaze, educate and empower artists and audiences in order to make the Cleveland public a more conscious and compassionate community.

> Esperanza, Inc.: To enhance educational opportunities for Hispanic Americans.

> Visiting Nurse Association: The Visiting Nurse Association of Cleveland provides innovative, high quality, and cost effective community health services to all people by: delivering care that promotes health, independence, and dignity; teaching people to care for themselves and each other; and providing services to the needy as funds permit.

Elements of the Plan

The strategic plan describes how the organization will achieve its mission. It indicates who will be served, how they will be served, and how the organization will support itself financially. The strategy must be based on solid information about the needs of the community and the clients and constituents being served. The strategic plan should also include a process for evaluating the value and effectiveness of the programs and services.

Fundamental to a good plan is a proposal for solid financial structure, including the costs of providing services and the key sources of revenue. The viability of revenue sources should be assessed, and alternative revenue opportunities to be cultivated should be proposed. Unfortunately, too many organizations create plans without addressing the revenue model.

Measurement

Measurement is critical for a few reasons. First, the chief executive, as well as the staff and board, need to be aware of how the organization is doing in order to adjust planning and implementation accordingly, especially given the dynamic nature of the environment. Second, measures of organizational progress give the board a way to see how the nonprofit is doing without getting in the chief executive's way. The board needs answers to questions such as these: How are we doing? Where are we achieving success? Where are we having difficulties? How will you, the chief executive, remedy any problems or overcome obstacles? And, how can we, the board, help? These questions should, in effect, be asked at every board meeting. In order to have this discussion, the chief executive needs to have good and credible measurement systems in place, quarterly reporting to the board, and continuous planning processes to adjust to changes good and bad.

As noted previously, measurement can be difficult and expensive for nonprofits. It is in fact quite daunting for an organization to document the long-term effects of certain programs and services. Short-term, concrete effects, such as participation rates, can be measured, and other short-term effects can be assessed by using instruments such as surveys and focus groups. It is incumbent on the chief executive and the staff to develop a measurement system in order to document for the board and key stakeholders the organization's progress and impact.

Gathering, Synthesizing, and Presenting Information

In order to continuously assess and update the organization's relevance and impact, the chief executive must establish an organizational process to gather information about the priority needs of clients; the quality and value of each key service; the potential volatility of each revenue source; possible new revenue sources; each key funder's expectations of the organization; the caliber and scope of work that is being done by other organizations that serve the same constituents; best practices in the field; failing practices in the field; and possibilities for strategic alliances.

Much of this information is readily accessible to people involved with the organization; a system simply needs to be established for organizing and reviewing the data. For example, program staff members and volunteers who provide direct services are sensitive to the most pressing needs and interests of clients as well as their feedback; this information can be augmented by client surveys and focus groups conducted by outside reviewers. Development officers should be keenly aware of the viability of key funding sources; members of the organization should seek additional input from funding experts in the field, current literature, and academic research institutions. Staff members responsible for accounting and financial reports should be alert to changes in revenue and expense patterns; financial consultants, or even board members with the necessary expertise, can assist the staff in analyzing financial information and developing financial strategies. With regard to best practices as well as failed practices in the field, national and regional conferences and literature provide useful insights and perspectives. Thus, much of the essential information is already in the hands of the staff.

The chief executive should establish a procedure for systematically disseminating and analyzing this information. This process can include a combination of written reports (concise, well organized, with bullet points) as well as staff meetings and discussions. The exact procedure depends on the size and scope of the organization; it is easier for the key staff members of smaller organizations to convene and discuss and analyze information, whereas larger organizations may need to break the process down by departments or programs. The chief executive should determine what information is the most useful and necessary and then synthesize the information in order to gauge the organization's effectiveness, impact, and financial health and viability.

The chief executive is responsible for alerting the board when there is a change in the wind with regard to any key matter. When presenting this information to the board, the chief executive should give a clear summary of the issues and their implications, alternative courses of action, and recommendations. Usually, the recommendations focus on averting or remedying a threat, capitalizing on an opportunity, or updating the organization to ensure its relevance, impact, and sustainability.

Balancing Imagination and Iteration

The chief executive must make sure the organization is effectively serving the community on a daily basis by making small, incremental adjustments, and she or he must also be able to imagine the future on a larger scale. The chief executive has to use all the different kinds of information available—client needs and issues, staff concerns and insights, board members' observations and interests, funders' interests, and changes in the broader environment—to look at the whole organization and to envision new ways of achieving results.

In the early 1990s, Brian Holley, the executive director of the Cleveland Botanical Garden, had a grand vision to build a great new facility, designed by a world-class architect, to house two natural environments—a desert and a jungle. The site would be designed to educate children and adults about the planet and its natural resources. The board had hired Holley because of his outstanding experience, had enticed him to move from Toronto to Cleveland, and then empowered him to make his vision a reality. Holley drew on the organization's assets, particularly the generous families that had demonstrated their commitment to the Botanical Garden for generations. He leveraged the interests of these families as well as public funding and foundation grants for educating the city's children. Only eight years later, the Cleveland Botanical Garden had surpassed its capital-campaign goal, engaged Graham Gund to build its magnificent new site, and completed the project ahead of time and under budget. Additionally, the Cleveland Botanical Garden expanded its local school outreach programs, broadened its educational offerings to include environmental and conservation research, and established international partnerships, while continuing to offer a wide array of local gardening classes to its long-term devotees. The board and its leadership joined Holley in dreaming, and they made the dream happen in a difficult fundraising environment in a city that is losing some of its most substantial corporate benefactors. It took focus, attention, and hard work, but they started by imagining.

The Cleveland Botanical Garden is an example of boldness, imagination, and vision. It is also an example of iterative planning. Throughout the eight years in which Holley led the implementation, he adjusted the organization's plans numerous times—with board and staff input—in order to adapt to changes in funding; changes were made on the basis of architectural requirements, the relative educational value of certain exhibits, the relevance of program content given changes in environmental and ecological sciences, and relationships with various organizational partners such as schools, senior residential sites, and other community centers.

To borrow from a for-profit example, Zuzka is a highly creative and entrepreneurial woman who emigrated from Czechoslovakia to New York in the late 1980s. At the age of thirty, trying to find a way to apply her abilities to a profession in her new country, she evaluated her assets: she was a highly talented fabric artist, and she had a small storehouse of hand-dyed fabrics from India that she had brought with her when she came to the United States. Her idea was to use the beautiful fabrics to make elegant and unique pillows for people's homes. She pulled out the yellow pages and began to call retailers that sold high-end home furnishings. Eventually, she called a company that had a number of successful shops. When Zuzka described her pillows, the woman at the other end of the line said that she was the daughter of the owner and that they were meeting that very day for a strategic-planning retreat; the woman suggested that Zuzka bring her pillows to the meeting. Zuzka hung up the phone, called a few friends, and said, "Hurry over. We have to make pillows!" Zuzka made the pillows that day and presented them. The company bought the full line, and today Zuzka's fashion designs are presented at international shows in Milan, are sold in the finest stores in the world, and are favored by film and television stars.

For most nonprofit executives, the story of making pillows resonates. Like Zuzka, chief executives of nonprofits also have to be nimble according to the market; they know that if they are not able to pull together raw materials and move quickly and adeptly, they will miss out. One key distinction, however, is that all activities of the nonprofit organization must be mission-related. Additionally, nonprofit executives need to keep their boards involved regarding strategic opportunities. At the same time, boards need to understand that the nonprofits that thrive are assessing and responding to opportunities and challenges on a continual basis. Adaptability is a key ingredient for organizational success.

The Bottom Line

Both imagination and planning are so essential to success that they need to be built into the fabric of the entire organization and to be part of ongoing discussions among board members and staff. The chief executive, as the chief planning officer, must track and monitor progress, continuously assess community needs, and explore new opportunities. The board's role is to support the chief executive in order to achieve organizational dreams. The board can join the chief executive in being bold and visionary, continuously updating itself and adapting to new circumstances.

Nonprofits are magnets for support when they dream bold visions and build a process for rigorous, continuous planning into the fabric of their organizations.

10

Volunteerism as a Powerful New Force

*The global economy compels a broader conception
of community and of business leadership in it. . . .
It should be equated not simply with money, but with
involvement in activities that contribute to the quality of
life. It should include people of all levels from companies
that differ in size, industry, and geographic scope.*

*As traditional sources of leadership dry up, com-
munities must welcome and adjust to new sources of
civic talent.*
—Rosabeth Moss Kanter, World Class, 1995

Nonprofits are struggling to meet the complex needs and address
the interests of vast and diverse constituents; businesses have
a growing interest in volunteerism. This is a moment of tremendous
opportunity. Nonprofits are advancing on the path of entrepreneurship and innovation, businesses are answering the call of service, and the emerging Millennial Generation shows signs of
becoming a powerful service force.

Because of current fiscal pressures, nonprofits are reorienting
themselves. They are achieving success by adopting business practices that are relevant and useful. Nonprofits are establishing fee-for-
services programs, designing effective communications to make clear
cases for support among key constituent groups, focusing services for

increased impact, measuring outcomes, and forming strategic alliances. Lester Salamon, the nation's leading nonprofit researcher, explains that "in the face of . . . fiscal pressures, nonprofit organizations managed to expand their activities in response to growing demand. . . . Furthermore, this was achieved with little reported adverse impact on disadvantaged clients and customers" (2004, p. 3).

Furthermore, nonprofits now have access to a new pool of volunteer talent as employers of all sizes recognize that community involvement is good for business, good for employees, and good for the community. According to management expert Rosabeth Moss Kanter,

> In the global economy, community service has become another set of weapons in the strategic arsenal, more intimately connected with the business mission, more highly integrated with a variety of business foundations, and sometimes not even local in scope. . . . The one goal for community service . . . is employee relations: supporting employees who live in a community in their service to it [and] making them feel proud to work for the company because of what it contributes to local quality of life. . . . [The company's] status as a world class knowledge center is maintained because of community amenities attractive to knowledge workers, including educational excellence, cultural events, and innovative social enterprise, all of which require active civic engagement [1995, p. 191].

Because businesses now see the value of community involvement, they encourage and support employees who volunteer.

The Millennials Are Coming

The momentum for volunteerism shows signs of escalating. The volunteer labor force is likely to expand as the Millennial generation, born in or following 1982, is emerging into the workforce with a heightened sense of community responsibility.

> As a group, Millennials are unlike any other youth generation in living memory. They are more numerous, more affluent, better educated, and more ethnically diverse. More important, they are beginning to manifest a wide array of positive social habits that older Americans no longer associate with youth, including a new focus on teamwork, achievement, modesty, and good conduct. Only a few years from now, this can-do youth revolution will overwhelm the cynics and pessimists. Over the next decade, the Millennial Generation will entirely recast the image of youth from downbeat and alienated to upbeat and engaged—with potentially seismic consequences for America [Howe and Strauss, 2000, p. 4].

The maturation of the Millennials, then, is another factor that will feed volunteerism and enhance the opportunity to improve communities.

Multiculturalism

Community service is a force that will foster multiculturalism and an increased appreciation and understanding of diverse communities. As our nation's neighborhoods become even more balkanized, with people living among neighbors who are not like themselves, volunteerism allows citizens from a variety of backgrounds to come together to address matters of mutual interest (Brooks, 2004, p. 48). Nonprofit organizations become magnets for people who are interested in a variety of issues ranging from heart disease to performing arts to higher education to hospice care. Through volunteerism, people have great opportunities to cross ethnic, racial, and socio-economic borders to improve society for all.

The Global Scale of Service

Interest in community service is expanding globally, and a number of new initiatives are being established to engage people in philanthropy and volunteerism throughout the world. Idealist.org, formed by Ami Dar, is an international volunteer-matching service. The Clarence Foundation was formed in San Francisco to support individuals seeking to make global financial contributions. Through service, Americans will learn about other nations and cultures and their needs; expanding international volunteerism and philanthropy presents extraordinary opportunities for deepening our understanding of international affairs.

International businesses are encouraging volunteerism as well. Citigroup has established an internal service to facilitate employee volunteerism throughout the world. With 275,000 employees in over a hundred countries, Citigroup can make a significant impact on the scope of services and on international communications and understanding.

A Lever to Move the World

This century brings great new opportunities for civic engagement. Citizens involved in meaningful and productive service enhance knowledge and understanding and improve the human condition.

> The only hope we have ever had has always been out in front of us, leading and guiding us to a place where neither we nor anyone else has ever been before. The good life is not to be found wrapped up and waiting for us like the Dead Sea Scrolls or some ancient artifacts from a culture that once flourished but is now long gone. Not at all. The good life, whose object, like that of hope, is a future good, difficult but possible to obtain, enables us to

live now that which we seek. The direction is always forward. We can be instructed by the past, and remem-
brance is one of the most powerful engines that drives us
forward, but forward is the direction in which the engine
will move us [Gomes, 2002, p. 284].

A lever turns a small amount of force into a tremendous output.
Throughout the United States and the world, groups of people are
responding to new challenges and seeking new ways to improve their
communities. By working together, businesses and nonprofits can
leverage those small inputs of good will to produce an extraordinary
benefit for the world. Archimedes said that if he had a lever long
enough and a place to stand, he could change the world. The lever is
the good will of volunteers. The place to stand is here. The moment
is now.

References

Allende, I. *My Invented Country*. New York: HarperCollins, 2003.

Axelrod, R. *The Evolution of Cooperation*. New York: Basic Books, 1984.

Bennis, W. G. "The Seven Ages of the Leader." *Harvard Business Review*, Jan. 2004, p. 46.

Bowen, W. G. "When a Business Leader Joins a Nonprofit Board." *Harvard Business Review*, Sept. 1994, pp. 4–8.

BPAmocoAlive: Environmental and Social Update. London, England: BP Amoco, 2003.

Brooks, D. "Our Sprawling, Supersize Utopia." *New York Times, Magazine Desk*, Apr. 4, 2004, pp. 46–51.

BVU Survey of Board Candidates Elected Through BVU. Cleveland: Business Volunteers Unlimited, 2002–2003.

Center for Corporate Citizenship. "Community Involvement Index 2003." Chestnut Hill, Mass.: Center for Corporate Citizenship at Boston College, 2003.

Code of Ethical Principles and Standards of Professional Practice. Alexandria, Va.: Association of Fundraising Professionals, 2002.

Cone, C. L., Feldman, M. A., and DaSilva, A. T. "Causes and Effects." *Harvard Business Review*, July 2003, pp. 95–101.

Drucker, P. F. "Managing Knowledge Means Managing Oneself." *Leader to Leader*, Spring 2000, pp. 8–10.

Gardner, J. W. *Living, Leading, and the American Dream*. San Francisco: Jossey-Bass, 2003.

Goethe, J. W., von. *Faust* (J. Anster, trans.). (Originally published 1835.) Available at http://www.goethesociety.org/pages/quotescom.html.

Gomes, P. J. *The Good Life: Truths That Last in Times of Need*. New York: HarperCollins, 2002.

Gregorian, V. Keynote speech at the 20th anniversary conference, Independent Sector, Washington, D.C., Oct. 2000.

Hess, D., Rogovsky, N., and Dunfee, T. W. "The Next Wave of Corporate Community Involvement: Corporate Social Initiatives." *California Management Review,* Winter 2002, pp. 110–125.

Hoffman, E. *Lost in Translation.* New York: Penguin Books, 1989.

Howe, F. *Welcome to the Board: Your Guide to Effective Participation.* San Francisco: Jossey-Bass, 1995.

Howe, N., and Strauss, W. *Millennials Rising: The Next Great Generation.* New York: Vintage Books, 2000.

Illinois Nonprofits: Building Capacity for the Next Century. St. Paul, Minn.: Illinois Facilities Fund and the Donors Forum of Chicago, 1998.

Klein, D. S. "Who Am I." *SBN Magazine,* July 2002, p. 40.

Korngold, A., and Voudouris, E. "Corporate Volunteerism: Strategic Community Involvement." In D. Burlingham and D. Young (eds.), *Corporate Philanthropy at the Crossroads.* Bloomington and Indianapolis: Indiana University Press, 1996.

Lang, E. M. "Voluntarism and the Human Spirit." In *Volunteerism: The Directory of Organizations, Training, Programs and Publications.* (3rd ed.) New Providence, N.J.: Bowker, 1991.

Langley, M., "Finishing Touch—Nonprofit Broker Puts Corporate Hotshots onto Charitable Boards; New Trustees Get a Boost Back at Work, Thanks to Business Matchmaker; the Ousting of 'Big Tooth.'" *Wall Street Journal,* Sept. 17, 1999, p. 1.

Leifer, J. C., and Glomb, M. B. *Legal Obligations of Nonprofit Boards: A Guidebook for Board Members.* Washington, D.C.: National Center for Nonprofit Boards, 1997.

Masaoka, J. "The Effectiveness Trap." *Stanford Social Innovation Review,* Spring 2003, pp. 82–83.

McCullough, D. *John Adams.* New York: Simon & Schuster, 2001.

McFarlan, F. W. "Working on Nonprofit Boards: Don't Assume the Shoe Fits." *Harvard Business Review,* Nov.–Dec. 1999, pp. 65–80.

Moss Kanter, R. *World Class: Thriving Locally in a Global Economy.* New York: Simon & Schuster, 1995.

The New Nonprofit Almanac IN BRIEF. Washington, D.C.: INDEPENDENT SECTOR, 2001.

The Nonprofit Governance Index. Washington, D.C.: National Center for Nonprofit Boards and the Stanford University Graduate School of Business, 2000.

Peters, J., and Wolfred, T. *Daring to Lead: Nonprofit Executive Directors and Their Work Experience*. San Francisco: CompassPoint, 2001.

Porter, M. E. *Corporate Philanthropy: Taking the High Ground*. New York: Foundation Strategy Group, 2003.

Responding to the Leadership Challenge: Findings of a CEO Survey on Global Corporate Citizenship. Geneva, Switzerland: World Economic Forum and the Prince of Wales International Business Leaders Forum, 2002.

Royal, W. "Doing Good Can Mean Big Headaches." *New York Times*, Nov. 17, 2002, p. 12.

Ruiz Patton, S. "Bush Aide Applauds Cleveland Program." *Plain Dealer* [Cleveland, Ohio], June 3, 2003, p. B5.

Salamon, L. M. *America's Nonprofit Sector: A Primer*. (2nd ed.) New York: Foundation Center, 1999.

Salamon, L. M., and O'Sullivan, R. *Stressed but Coping: Nonprofit Organizations and the Current Fiscal Crisis*. Baltimore: Johns Hopkins University Center for Civil Society Studies, 2004.

Thomas, M. T. "Leading by Feel." *Harvard Business Review*, Jan. 2004, p. 27.

"2002 Business Leadership Forum Monograph." Presented at the 10th Annual Awards for Excellence in Corporate Community Services, Business Leadership Forum, San Francisco, Mar. 2002.

Vargas Llosa, M. "Why Literature? From the New Republic." In S. J. Gould and R. Atwan (eds.), *The Best American Essays*. Boston: Houghton Mifflin, 2002.

Index